T0006431

LIVE on purpose

100 DEVOTIONS

FOR LETTING GO OF FEAR

AND FOLLOWING GOD

SADIE ROBERTSON HUFF

WITH TAMA FORTNER

THOMAS NELSON
Since 1798

Live on Purpose

© 2021 Sadie Robertson Huff

Portions of this book are taken from *Live* (978-1-4002-1306-1; © 2020) and *Live Fearless* (978-1-4003-0939-9; © 2018).

Tommy Nelson, PO Box 141000, Nashville, TN 37214

All rights reserved. No portion of this book may be reproduced, stored in a retrieval system, or transmitted in any form or by any means—electronic, mechanical, photocopy, recording, scanning, or other—except for brief quotations in critical reviews or articles, without the prior written permission of the publisher.

Published in Nashville, Tennessee, by Tommy Nelson. Tommy Nelson is an imprint of Thomas Nelson. Thomas Nelson is a registered trademark of HarperCollins Christian Publishing, Inc.

Tama Fortner is represented by Cyle Young of C.Y.L.E. (Cyle Young Literary Elite, LLC), a literary agency.

Unless otherwise noted, Scripture quotations are taken from the Holy Bible, New International Version®, NIV®. Copyright © 1973, 1978, 1984, 2011 by Biblica, Inc.® Used by permission of Zondervan. All rights reserved worldwide. www.zondervan.com. The "NIV" and "New International Version" are trademarks registered in the United States Patent and Trademark Office by Biblica, Inc.® Scripture quotations marked AMP are taken from the Amplified® Bible (AMP). Copyright © 2015 by The Lockman Foundation. Used by permission. www.Lockman.org. Scripture quotations marked MSG are taken from THE MESSAGE. Copyright © 1993, 2002, 2018 by Eugene H. Peterson. Used by permission of NavPress. All rights reserved. Represented by Tyndale House Publishers, a Division of Tyndale House Ministries. Scripture quotations marked NASB are taken from the New American Standard Bible® (NASB). Copyright © 1960, 1962, 1963, 1968, 1971, 1972, 1973, 1975, 1977, 1995 by The Lockman Foundation. Used by permission. www.Lockman.org. Scripture quotations marked NCV are taken from the New Century Version®. Copyright © 2005 by Thomas Nelson. Used by permission. All rights reserved. Scripture quotations marked NKJV are taken from the New King James Version®. Copyright © 1982 by Thomas Nelson. Used by permission. All rights reserved. Scripture quotations marked NLT are taken from the Holy Bible, New Living Translation. Copyright © 1996, 2004, 2015 by Tyndale House Foundation. Used by permission of Tyndale House Ministries, Carol Stream, Illinois 60188. All rights reserved. Scripture quotations marked TPT are taken from The Passion Translation®. Copyright © 2017, 2018 by Passion & Fire Ministries, Inc. Used by permission. All rights reserved. ThePassionTranslation.com.

ISBN 978-1-4002-1312-2 (audiobook)
ISBN 978-1-4002-1311-5 (eBook)
ISBN 978-1-4002-1309-2 (HC)
ISBN 978-0-310-13605-7 (Walmart)

Library of Congress Cataloging-in-Publication Data

Names: Huff, Sadie Robertson, 1997- author. | Fortner, Tama, 1969- author.
Title: Live on purpose : 100 devotions for letting go of fear and following God / Sadie Robertson Huff with Tama Fortner.
Description: Nashville, Tennessee : Thomas Nelson, [2021] | Includes bibliographical references. | Audience: Ages 13-16 | Summary: "Live on Purpose, Sadie Robertson's confidence-inspiring devotional based on her bestselling books Live Fearless and Live, offers intention in your everyday time with God and helps you make the most of your amazing, one-of-a-kind life"-- Provided by publisher.
Identifiers: LCCN 2021011611 (print) | LCCN 2021011612 (ebook) | ISBN 9781400213092 (hardcover) | ISBN 9781400213115 (epub)
Subjects: LCSH: Christian teenagers--Religious life. | Fear--Religious aspects--Christianity. | BISAC: YOUNG ADULT NONFICTION / Religious / Christian / Devotional & Prayer | YOUNG ADULT NONFICTION / Social Topics / Values & Virtues
Classification: LCC BV4531.3 .H84 2021 (print) | LCC BV4531.3 (ebook) | DDC 242/.63--dc23
LC record available at https://lccn.loc.gov/2021011611
LC ebook record available at https://lccn.loc.gov/2021011612

Photography copyright © Angela Groce

Printed in the United States of America

24 25 26 27 28 LBC 11 10 9 8 7

Contents

1

On Purpose and with a Purpose

I am certain that God, who began the good work within you, will continue his work until it is finally finished on the day when Christ Jesus returns.

PHILIPPIANS 1:6 NLT

DO YOU EVER WONDER, *WHY? WHY AM I here in this place at this time?* I think that's something everyone wonders at one time or another. I know I did. Everywhere we turn in this world, something is telling us we don't quite measure up and we don't really matter all that much anyway.

If you're searching for the truth about *who* you are and *why* you are, here it is: we're all here because God created us. We're not some random accident of molecules and evolution. We are "fearfully and wonderfully made" (Psalm 139:14). We're "marvelous" (NLT) and "amazing" (NCV). And not just *we* as in all of humankind, but you specifically. God made *you* wonderful, marvelous, and amazing. And He made you *on purpose*.

God didn't stop there, though. He made you on purpose and *with a purpose*. That purpose has nothing to do with money, clothes, skin color, family background, or how many likes you get on Instagram or TikTok. God's purpose for each of us is to love others and point them back to Him and His love. *Boom!* Stop and read that again. *That* is your purpose. It's not some faraway, mysterious thing you'll arrive at someday—it's here and now.

How you live out this purpose is as individual as you are. But don't worry, God's got it all planned out. In fact, He's had it planned right from the start: "For we are God's masterpiece. He has created us anew in Christ Jesus, so we can do the good things he planned for us long ago" (Ephesians 2:10 NLT). All you have to do to step into His purpose for your life is follow Him. Say yes to Him today and every day, no matter what. Because God's purpose is for all the seasons and circumstances of your life—the good times, the storms, the struggles, the heartbreaking times, the growing times, and the quiet times.

Don't wait until you get your act together or you get it all figured out. Step into the life God is calling you to live now. You won't regret it. And that's a promise—not from me but from God.

Holy Father, today I declare that I will
live my life for You. Lead me forward in the
purpose You have planned for me. Amen.

2

The "Group Text" Call

God saved us and called us to live a holy life. He did this, not because we deserved it, but because that was his plan from before the beginning of time—to show us his grace through Christ Jesus.

2 TIMOTHY 1:9 NLT

YOU CAN'T HANG AROUND CHRISTIANS FOR long without hearing someone talk about their *calling* or being *called* by God. And you might wonder, *What on earth does that mean? Have I been called?*

Let me answer the second question first: *Yes!* You've been called. Every single person on this planet has been called to say yes to Jesus. To love, follow, and obey Him. It's like God sent out a group text to the whole world because "He does not want anyone to be lost" (2 Peter 3:9 NCV).

I was thirteen when I answered that call. I was playing basketball overseas for the Junior Olympics, and it was the first time in my life I'd really been away from my parents. I didn't know the girls on the team very well. And because they were halfway around the world from their parents, I guess they thought they could do pretty much anything they wanted—so they did. What they wanted wasn't good, and it included things that thirteen-year-old me had yet to see. Joining in just didn't feel right in my spirit. I knew I wanted to follow Jesus instead.

I talk about this in my book *Live*, and I want to remind you here that in life you *do* have options, even when it doesn't feel like it. People often give in to temptation because they think if everyone else is doing something, then they have to as well. Not true. When I was overseas, showing up at all of those parties was mandatory, so I didn't have the option to skip them—but I *did* have the option to not participate. I literally sat by the door and waited until the party was over. I just knew the whole time that Jesus was greater, and I wanted to follow Him. That summer I was baptized by my dad and started answering God's call on my life.

That was the first step—answering that call. I encourage you to respond to that call too if you haven't already. Give your life to Jesus. Now, you might be sitting there thinking, *I'm young. I have my whole life to respond to the call of God.* But if you respond today, think of how much more time you'll have to impact the world around you for Him. But first you have to answer the call.

———————————

Lord, thank You for this call You've placed on my life. Teach me what it means to say, "Yes, Lord!" Amen.

3

The "It's for You" Call

I heard the voice of the Lord saying, "Whom shall I send? And who will go for us?" And I said, "Here am I. Send me!"

ISAIAH 6:8

IN ADDITION TO THE WORLDWIDE "GROUP text" call we talked about on page 8, there's a personal call that everyone gets.

Mine came at a conference when a woman named Alex Seeley stepped up to preach. I was seventeen, going into my senior year, and wondering what to do with my life. As Alex preached, I thought, *Everything she's saying matters because it's from the Word of God. If I'm going to influence people, I want to say something that matters.* That was my first glimpse of my personal calling. God was calling me to preach and tell my generation about His amazing, unending love.

Let me say that you'll see people who inspire and lead you toward your calling. But you aren't called to *be* someone else— even if your callings look similar. I find my purpose by speaking truth over people's lives, just as Alex does. But we'll touch way more people if we each run in the lane God has set before us. *Your* calling is original.

Shortly after I heard Alex preach, a mentor said to me, "I want to encourage you with the word *hineni*." *Hineni* means "Here I am, God"—with no limits and no distractions. It's the word used by Abraham, Samuel, and Moses when they responded to God's call on their lives. I listened, but I wasn't ready to fully trust God to send me wherever He wanted.

Fast-forward to a few years later when I was visiting a church called The Belonging Co. I was shocked to see Alex Seeley walk up to preach. Instead of sharing her prepared message, she said, "I feel like somebody needs to hear something very specific. The word is *hineni*." Alex went on to say, "If you recently prayed, 'Here I am, God,' but you still have limits or distractions, you need to let go of your safety net and really let Him send you."

Y'all, I felt like the whole church and God Himself was look-ing at me!

Up to that point, I'd never really trusted God enough to step away from my safety nets. After that moment, though, everything shifted. I let go of the boyfriend who wasn't right for me, left a secure job, and stepped into the unknown.

Do you need to let go of some safety nets? Are you ready to say, "Here I am, God. Send me"?

Holy Father, let my prayer every morning be, "Here I am. Send me!" Amen.

4

Faith for the Vision

Immediately Jesus reached out his hand and caught him.
"You of little faith," he said, "why did you doubt?"

MATTHEW 14:31

IT WAS ALMOST 2020, AND AS CLASSIC
millennial believers, my husband Christian and I were sitting
in the Chick-fil-A drive-thru, talking about our "word" for the
new year.

"Babe," I said, "we need a good word to focus on for the year
because what we focused on this last year was so challenging
and powerful."

Christian looked over at me and proudly said, "I'm going with
vision."

Now, I have a little bit of my dad's personality in me, so I like
to be a challenger in some situations. I was sitting there, trying
to let my husband have his word and be excited about it. And
don't get me wrong; it's a great word to focus on. But I was also
thinking, *Okay, I need to give just a little pushback.*

I said, "Look, vision is great. I love it. I hope for vision too. But let me ask you this: You've been telling me all about the vision that God's given you, and we've been talking about the vision we have together. Do you *really* feel like you need *more* vision in 2020?"

Christian sat there for a minute. "You're right," he said. "Let me think about it a little bit longer."

Another week went by, and we were at a Passion Conference when Christian said, "I've got my word! It's *faith*! I realized you were right. We have a lot of vision, and now I think what we really need is faith for the vision."

Now, that's powerful! *Faith* for the vision!

I have always been gripped by Peter's faith in Matthew 14, even though he became fearful moments after stepping out of the boat. I think it's because his faith had him stepping out of the boat, even when he didn't know what would happen next. So often we want God to show us the finished picture of His vision for us *before* we step out of our boat. But God doesn't usually reveal the full vison. What He does give us is His Word, and through His Word, He gives us faith (Romans 10:17).

Will you choose to let His Word give you the faith to step into the unknown, into His vision for your life? Because if you're willing to do that, you're going to be used by God in the most extraordinary ways.

———————————

Lord, fill me with the faith to step
into Your vision for my life. Amen.

5

The Runaway

The Lord spoke his word to Jonah son of Amittai: "Get up, go to the great city of Nineveh, and preach against it, because I see the evil things they do."

JONAH 1:1–2 NCV

WHEN GOD PUTS A SPECIFIC CALL, OR PURPOSE, on our lives, He doesn't force us to accept it. We have some choices about how we'll respond. We could say, "Here I am. Send me!"

Or we could be like Jonah and run away.

Jonah very clearly heard the call of God: *Go to Nineveh and preach.* But Jonah didn't want to go to Nineveh, so he jumped on a ship headed in the opposite direction. Of course, God didn't give up on Jonah. He kept repeating that call on Jonah's life. And God was *not* letting Jonah off the hook—so much so that God sent a big fish to swallow him. (Wild, I know!) After three days, the fish spit him out, and this time Jonah headed for Nineveh. I probably would too if I'd just been swallowed by a fish.

Some of us are like Jonah. We've received a calling from God.

We feel like we know what He wants us to do. But the thought of actually going out and doing it is so scary and overwhelming that we say, "I think I must have heard You wrong, God." Then we turn around and run the other way.

Here's the thing: it's not possible to outrun God. Jonah couldn't, and neither can we. God is chasing after us but in the best possible way: with love. Psalm 23 says it this way: "Surely your goodness and unfailing love will pursue me all the days of my life" (v. 6 NLT).

Nothing will ever separate us from the love God has for us (Romans 8:38–39). We can ignore it, and we can pretend it's not real. But God's love for us and His calling on our lives will still be there, no matter how far or fast we might try to run away. Sure, you can keep saying no, and you can keep running. But God's call will always be there for you to face. The purpose He has for you—that He chose for you before the foundation of the world—does not just go away. Follow God wherever He leads you.

Holy Father, open my heart, my mind, and my spirit to the calling You've placed on my life. And help me to boldly accept it. Amen.

6

The "Prove It"

Gideon replied, "If you are truly going to help me, show me a sign to prove that it is really the Lord speaking to me."

JUDGES 6:17 NLT

WHEN FACED WITH A CALLING FROM GOD, some people run away. Others look God in the eye (figuratively speaking, of course) and say, "Prove it."

Gideon did that. In Judges 6, when the angel of the Lord said Gideon would lead Israel to victory over the Midianites, he was *hiding* from the Midianites in a winepress so he could thresh his wheat. Not exactly a mighty warrior. Maybe that's why God was patient when Gideon asked for not one but *two* signs to prove this calling. First, Gideon laid out a fleece and said to God, "In the morning, make the fleece wet with dew and the ground around it dry." So God did. Next, Gideon said, "Okay, make the fleece dry and the ground around it wet with dew." Again, God did exactly as Gideon asked. And finally, Gideon had enough proof to believe.

I've got to be honest; I've asked for signs too. Once, I was dating this guy I knew I shouldn't be dating. So I said to God, "If You really want me to break up with him, give me a sign." That weekend we went on a date, and the guy literally ran into a stop sign. No joke. *Okay, God. Noted.*

While it's not wrong to ask for signs, we need to be careful. If we're not sure what God's will is in a situation, that's one thing. But if we start asking God to jump through hoops to prove who He is, that's completely different. And if you believe you've been given a sign, make sure it's really from God. I mean, not everything is a sign. Your "fleece" might be wet because somebody tripped and spilled water on it. Make sure any sign agrees with God's Word, then talk to trusted mentors and keep on praying. I've found that we tend to overcomplicate who God is and how He speaks. Remember that His love is uncomplicated. If it's truly a message from God, He'll make it clear.

I'm not saying to never ask for signs, but the truth is, we don't really need them. God's voice—through His Word and His Spirit living inside us—is enough. Just know that if you do pray for a sign, you just might run into one.

Holy Father, forgive me for ever asking You to prove Yourself. Instead, open my eyes to see all the wonderful ways You already show up in my life. Amen.

7

The Half Listener

"For I know the plans I have for you," declares the Lord, "plans to prosper you and not to harm you, plans to give you hope and a future."

JEREMIAH 29:11

SOME PEOPLE HEAR THE CALL OF GOD IN their lives, and they *sort of* listen. They *sort of* obey. But not really. Mostly, they do what they really wanted to do all along.

Take King Saul. God told him to take out the Amalekites and destroy everything that belonged to them (1 Samuel 15:1–3). But instead, Saul and his men spared the king and "kept the best of the sheep and goats, the cattle, the fat calves, and the lambs" (1 Samuel 15:9 NLT). So basically, Saul only destroyed the stuff he and his army didn't think was worth keeping. Saul sort of obeyed, but not really.

And because Saul didn't fully obey God, he didn't get to experience the fullness of God's plans for his life. He eventually lost his place as king of Israel.

I first moved to Nashville because I felt God calling me to get out of my comfort zone. When I was offered a speaking opportunity on a tour based out of the city, I knew God was leading me there. The funny thing is, once I got to Nashville, I stayed in my comfort zone. I didn't challenge myself to fully obey what I knew God had put in me to do. It took that *hineni* moment that we talked about earlier (page 11) to get me moving again.

Here's what I want you to know: God is *so* good. He's *so* kind. If you don't respond to the call He has on your life, I'm not saying He's going to strike you down or send a big fish to swallow you. But from what I know about God, He is going to keep pouring people, events, and things into your life, trying to get you to hear Him and to know how much He loves you. And until you answer His call, you're going to miss out on all the amazing things He has planned to do with you and for you in this life.

More than that, though, you're going to miss out on the fullness of a life lived with Him—the love, joy, and peace of walking with God. That's better than anything this world has to offer you, and that is what you'll receive when you walk in the center of His will for your life.

Don't just half listen to God. Don't just sort of obey. Go all in with Him. You won't regret it.

Holy Father, help me to fully listen,
fully obey, and fully follow You. Amen.

8

The "Who, Me?"

Moses said to God, "Who am I that I should go to Pharaoh and bring the Israelites out of Egypt?"

EXODUS 3:11

HAVE YOU EVER BEEN CALLED ON BY A teacher, coach, or boss and asked to do something you didn't think you were qualified to do? I bet you were so surprised that you looked back over your shoulder to see if there was someone else they could've possibly been talking to. It's that "Who, me?" moment.

Moses had one of those moments when God spoke to him through the burning bush. When God said He was sending Moses to Pharaoh to lead the Israelites out of Egypt, Moses' first response was, "Who am I to appear before Pharaoh? Who am I to lead the people of Israel out of Egypt?" (Exodus 3:11 NLT). Or in other words, "Who, me?"

Moses went on to name all the reasons why he couldn't do what God was calling him to do: *The people won't believe me* (4:1), *I'm no good at public speaking* (4:10), and *I just really don't want to go* (4:13).

Moses had a whole list of excuses and insecurities, but the real problem was that he thought God's call was about *him* and what *he* could do. It wasn't. God's call was about *Him* and what *He* could do.

We make that same mistake. I've done it myself so many times. I knew God was calling me to speak, but my excuse was, "God, I get so nervous in front of people. I have a hard time just reading out loud. How am I supposed to read the Bible in front of people?" And now look at what God has me doing.

Here's the thing I've learned: When God calls you to do something—especially if it's something you don't feel qualified to do—start praying and just say yes. God will equip you to do whatever He calls you to do. It probably won't be in an instant, but as you pray and as you trust God more than your fears, He will enable you and meet you where you are.

He definitely did that for me, and I have no doubt He'll do that for you too.

Lord, please show me the call You have placed on my life. I will trust You to help me answer that call. Amen.

9

The "I've Got This"

The LORD will work out his plans for my life—for your faithful love, O LORD, endures forever.

PSALM 138:8 NLT

HAVE YOU EVER HEARD PEOPLE SAY, "I'VE got this," when you know they really don't? I know I'm guilty of doing this. I cannot even tell you how many times I've tried to pick up something that's too heavy for me or I've taken on too much in a day. That's when my husband, Christian, gives me "the look," but I keep trying to prove that "I've got this."

We can be like that with God sometimes. We start to think we know more than He does about what's best for our lives— even though He's the one who made us and knows exactly what we need. It's called *pride*, and it can cause all kinds of trouble.

It certainly did for King Saul. Remember on page 18 when we talked about how God told Saul to destroy the Amalekites and everything that belonged to them, including their animals (1 Samuel 15:1–3)? Well, Saul didn't do that. And when the prophet Samuel confronted Saul about it, the king insisted he *had* obeyed God. I love what Samuel said next: "Then what is all the bleating of sheep and goats and the lowing of cattle I hear?" (1 Samuel 15:14 NLT). Busted!

That's when King Saul started trying to explain *his* plan. Instead of destroying the animals like God told him to, Saul was going to sacrifice them in worship of God. Wasn't that a better idea? *Nope.*

Thinking we have a better plan than God wasn't good then, and it's not good now. But we still do that sometimes, don't we? We'll be following along with God's plan, but then we see a way to make things easier—like Saul keeping all those animals. And we start thinking, *But, God, what if I did this instead? You probably didn't realize this option was available to me. And wouldn't this be a better plan?*

Um, no.

Here's the thing: God can see our lives from a much higher viewpoint than we can. He knows the past, present, and future and how everything fits together. We can trust that His plan is best—even if it doesn't make sense in the moment. We can't ever out-plan God. His plans are perfect, and they're perfect for us.

———————

Lord, forgive me for the times I try to follow my own plans instead of Yours. Show me where I need to make changes so that I am following Your path and not my own. Amen.

10

The Comparer

There are different ways that God works through people but the same God. God works in all of us in everything we do.

1 CORINTHIANS 12:6 NCV

COMPARISON IS SUCH A STRUGGLE IN OUR culture. With social media always at our fingertips, resisting the urge to measure ourselves against others is hard. We can even end up comparing our calling from God to what other people are doing for Him. And while it might seem like a bigger problem today, the "comparison" problem has been around for as long as people have been around. We can even see it in Peter's life.

Peter was one of the disciples closest to Jesus. They were bros. Peter followed Jesus for three years and saw Him do so many miraculous things. But when Jesus was arrested, Peter's fears took over, and he denied even knowing Jesus *three times*. After the resurrection, Jesus appeared to Peter at the Sea of Galilee and redeemed him *three times*. Then Jesus went on to tell Peter how He would use his life for God's glory. It was a beautiful, amazing, and grace-filled moment.

But right after that, Peter saw John and said, "What about him, Lord?" (John 21:21 NLT). Instead of focusing on the grace he'd been given, Peter wanted to compare his calling to John's. Would John's be better? Would it be easier?

So what was Jesus' answer? He looked at Peter and, without answering his question but speaking straight to his heart, said, "What is that to you? As for you, follow me" (v. 22 NLT).

Here's the thing: God has a specific purpose for your life. He may have already revealed it to you. He may have given you just a glimpse here and there. But no matter if you know your specific call or not, you can *always* know that we're all called to build the kingdom no matter where we are. He might ask you to do something big and bold in front of the world. Or it might be something behind the scenes. Don't compare callings. And don't ever think your calling is less (or more!) than someone else's. Because you can know this for certain: it's the perfect calling for you and for the glory of His kingdom.

Keep your focus on God and let your response to Him be, *Here I am, God. No limits, no distractions. Send me. Use me any way You want to use me.*

Holy Father, help me to keep my eyes
fixed on You and to say yes to the
plans You have for me. Amen.

11

The Overwhelmed

After the earthquake came a fire, but the Lord was not in the fire. And after the fire came a gentle whisper.

1 KINGS 19:12

WHETHER IT'S THE CRUSH OF DEADLINES, A massive test, or all the details of life, "overwhelm" happens. We can even get overwhelmed by our calling when we realize we're doing something we couldn't possibly do on our own.

Take Elijah, for example. With the power of God behind him, he took on wicked King Ahab, Queen Jezebel, *and* their 450 prophets of Baal (1 Kings 18:20–40). But when Elijah got word that Jezebel wanted him dead, he freaked. He ran for his life, lay under a bush, and said, "I have had enough, Lord" (1 Kings 19:4).

We do that too. We're following God, everything is exciting, and we see some success. But the minute somebody says, "This isn't going to work," we're like, "Oh yeah. You're probably right." And we tap out. Our fears and insecurities overwhelm us, and we want to quit.

But listen to how sweet God was to Elijah—because He'll

be just as sweet with you. God called Elijah to the top of Mount Horeb. There was a massive wind, an earthquake, and a fire. But God didn't speak through any of those big things. He spoke in a gentle whisper (1 Kings 19:11–13). God came and whispered to Elijah, and He'll do the same for you.

One time I heard pastor Craig Groeschel say, "When you draw near to God, he will draw near to you. . . . And if you'll be quiet and if you'll listen, you'll hear the gentle whisper of a good God, who is always with you."[1] That stuck with me.

When I was first asked to speak at the Passion Conference, I was humbled and completely overwhelmed. Just the year before, my friend Laney had asked if I thought I'd ever speak at Passion. I literally laughed! So, needless to say, I was shocked when I was asked the very next year. At first, that ask was so daunting to me, but I spent the year preparing and praying daily for God to give me the words to say. He whispered to me so many times during that year that, when it was time to speak, I wasn't overwhelmed. In fact, I couldn't wait to share!

Don't get overwhelmed by what God is calling you to do. Pray, soak in His Word, and listen for His whisper. His words will carry you through all that He's called you to do.

———————————

Lord, please quiet all the overwhelming noise in my life so that I can hear Your whispers. Amen.

12

The Look-Backer

[Jesus] gave his life to free us from every kind of sin, to cleanse us, and to make us his very own people, totally committed to doing good deeds.

TITUS 2:14 NLT

WE'VE ALL MADE MISTAKES. BUT WE CAN'T let those mistakes keep us from doing what God has called us to do. Yet that's exactly what happens for some of us. We know God wants to use us, but we look back at our mistakes and think, *I'm not good enough. God couldn't possibly use me.*

Not true! Actually, very far from true! Think about the Samaritan woman at the well in John 4. This lady had made a lot of mistakes over the years. She'd had five husbands and was living with guy number six. Her reputation was so shattered that she came to the well in the heat of the day when no one else would be there. Except someone *was* there: Jesus. And He asked her for a drink of water. Back then, that was a big deal. Jesus was a Jew, and Jews didn't speak to Samaritans. Period. What's more, men didn't speak to women in public, especially not women like her. Yet Jesus not only treated her with respect and kindness; He told her He was the Messiah. The woman ran to tell the whole village about Jesus, and because of her, many people believed. Even with all her mistakes, Jesus was able to use her to share the good news with the whole town.

So can God really use you? Absolutely!

There are so many people in the Bible who—by the world's standards—should have been disqualified from serving God. David committed adultery and murder. Saul hunted down Christians until Jesus turned him into a missionary. And just look at Jesus' family tree. You'll find a prostitute, a liar, and a cheat— also known as Rahab, Abraham, and Jacob.

Everybody has a past. Everybody has something they don't want the whole world to know. If we were disqualified from being used by God because of a bad past, then every person in the Bible except for Jesus would be gone. That's where the great love of God and what He did through Jesus comes in. When we decide to follow Him, God gives us grace, redemption, and a turning point so we can move forward and live for Jesus.

Don't look back at your mistakes and let them decide your future. God can still absolutely, 100 percent use you. He is just that good.

Holy God, wipe away the shame of my past and lead me into the future You would have me to live. Amen.

13

The Move Maker

May the Lord lead your hearts into a full understanding and
expression of the love of God and the patient endurance that
comes from Christ.

2 THESSALONIANS 3:5 NLT

OF ALL THE WAYS WE CAN RESPOND TO THE
call of God—running away, demanding proof, half listening—
being a "move maker" is the sweet spot.

Move makers are men and women of faith who are *moved*
by the Spirit of God and then *make moves* to impact the world
for the kingdom of God—not by their own strength or wisdom
but because the Holy Spirit is with them and the hand of God
is on them.

These are the people who hear God's call, put their faith and
trust in Him, and obey. In the Bible, they're people like Noah, who
not only listened when God said to build an ark but also grabbed
a hammer (Genesis 6). They're people like Mary, who heard the
angel's words and said, "I am the Lord's servant. May everything
you have said about me come true" (Luke 1:38 NLT). And they're

people like Ananias. When God told him to go to Saul—the man who had been terrorizing Christians—Ananias went (Acts 9).

Notice something about these people, though. Not one of them was perfect—even *after* they answered the call of God. Sure, Noah built the boat, but after the flood he planted a vineyard and got drunk with wine (Genesis 9). Mary became the mother of Jesus, but years later there was a time when she tried to get Him to stop teaching and come home (Mark 3). And when God told Ananias to go see Saul, Ananias was like, "Are You sure about that, God? You know who that guy is, right?" (Acts 9).

They made mistakes, but their obedience kept the kingdom of God moving forward. And that means you can be a move maker too. You aren't going to do everything perfectly, but that shouldn't stop you from doing what you can. Perfectionism is a bigger deal than we realize. It paralyzes us from simply being obedient. But you can decide to say, *Here I am, God, with no limits and no distractions.* Allow yourself to be moved by the Holy Spirit, and you will make a difference for His kingdom.

Holy Father, help me to put aside all the distractions and all the limits I've placed on You. Show me how to let You have full control of my life so that I can make a difference for You. Amen.

14

Before You're Ready

God is able to bless you abundantly, so that in all things at all times, having all that you need, you will abound in every good work.

2 CORINTHIANS 9:8

WHEN I STARTED GETTING ASKED TO SPEAK to groups, I didn't feel capable of speaking. And here's the truth: I actually wasn't.

The first time I showed up to speak at a church, I was so nervous. But I told myself, *Okay, I'm just going to do this*. I was supposed to speak for thirty minutes, but I only spoke for *five*— and the people asked for their money back. *True story.* At those first few speaking engagements, I would get so nervous onstage that I'd totally freeze. I would be like, "God loves you. Okay, bye!" Then I'd practically run off the stage. I was *so* awkward. But God didn't stop using me because I failed. He used those failures to train me.

Here's something you need to remember: *you will probably feel called before you feel ready*. Say yes anyway. If you try and fail, say yes again. Keep on saying yes to God. Every time you fall, get back up and try again. Why? Because when you fall in front of people, you'll get back up twice as fast.

Trust me, I've been in the spotlight since I was thirteen years old. I've had a lot of falls and fails. God is so grace-filled, and He kept picking me up and teaching me as we went on together. I survived those early days, I kept saying yes to God, and He used those experiences to train me. I can now confidently speak onstage because I have learned to be confident in God.

If you're feeling called to do something you don't feel ready to do, say yes anyway. Trust God to train you and teach you what you need to know. And if you fall, don't worry. God will pick you up and help you to say yes again to the purpose He has planned for you.

Holy Father, sometimes following You and Your call for my life is a scary thing. Please give me the courage to say yes anyway. Amen.

15

From Revelation
to Realization

God said to Noah, . . . "Make yourself an ark."

GENESIS 6:13–14 NKJV

REVELATION AND *REALIZATION* MIGHT LOOK
and sound like similar words, but there's a big difference in what
they mean. A *revelation* is something that you're suddenly aware
of—like you suddenly become aware of what God wants you to
do with your life (or at least part of it). A *realization* is when God
makes that revelation actually happen.

Chances are, you will have a *revelation* of what God wants
you to do before you see the *realization* of what He is going to do.

Think about Noah. God gave him a revelation: "You need to
build a boat." Noah listened. He acted on that revelation and
started building. And I bet he had some learning and training to
do before he figured out *exactly* how to build that boat. When the
rains started, Noah saw that God used the boat to save humankind and the animals. That's when the realization happened.

For me, I had a revelation that God wanted me to go on tour and speak to people about Him. Maybe I'd call it Live Original, but I wasn't sure. Back then, I never thought it would be what God has grown it to be. I never thought I'd speak at the Passion Conferences, go on to start a podcast, and spend every day working on content to preach, write, and encourage people in their faith.

That first revelation, though, was strong enough for me to know that I needed to start training and learning. I needed to stop listening to some of the music I was listening to, and I needed to stop watching some of the shows and movies I gave my time to. I needed to start digging deep into Scripture and saturate my life with the Word of God. I wouldn't know the Bible stories I know today if I had not spent that time in the Word—after I had the revelation, but before I had the realization.

When God gives you a revelation, that's your cue to ask Him to start teaching you what you need to know *before* you get to the realization. As He teaches and trains you, you'll not only learn what you need to know; you'll also learn to trust the Lord who leads you. And He'll lead you right into the purpose He has for your life.

Holy Father, open my eyes to see Your revelation for my life. Then teach me and train me so that I will be ready for the realization. Amen.

16

Like You're Five

"Truly I tell you, unless you change and become like little children, you will never enter the kingdom of heaven. Therefore, whoever takes the lowly position of this child is the greatest in the kingdom of heaven."

MATTHEW 18:3–4

WHEN I WAS FIVE, I GOT UP ON A TABLE AND started preaching to my parents. I sang a little jingle I had made up titled "Let's Give It Up for God," followed by an epic toe touch. I preached the truth I knew, unafraid and unashamed at five years old. I was simply in love with God, and I spoke a simple truth.

When our family's TV show took off, people started asking me to speak publicly, and as I mentioned before, fear gripped me. I feared what people thought of me way too much. I wondered if I was even qualified to be on a stage speaking. Somewhere between the time when I was five and my teenage years, I allowed other voices into my life—voices of self-doubt and a lack of faith and trust in God. Maybe you've felt the same way.

Do you remember the confidence you had when you were

little? What was it that stole your childlike boldness? Recapturing the confidence I had as a five-year-old took some time. It was a process, but I found it in the security of knowing who God made me to be. Start the process today. It will help you discover and live out your purpose.

I believe that when we're five, our confidence and freedom come from the voices around us and our parents' protection over who's allowed to speak into our lives. We hear voices of encouragement and voices of truth—voices telling us we are enough, we are beautiful just as we are, and we are loved.

Whether or not you had this growing up, there comes a point in life when you have to begin to do this for yourself. While parents protect for as long as they can, at some point you have to start protecting your own heart. Guard your heart, your ears, your eyes—and don't allow the world to take away the things that make you who you really are. Because what makes you uniquely who you are is what makes you real and what empowers you to truly live.

Having a child's perspective helps us prioritize what God says is most important. Today, let God redeem the confidence that you lost.

———————————

Lord, I pray that fear and shame would
have no authority over my life. Be a
shield around me, and protect me from
the voices that would silence my worship
and pull me away from You. Amen.

17

Altogether Beautiful

You are altogether beautiful, my darling, beautiful in every way.

SONG OF SOLOMON 4:7 NLT

HAVE YOU EVER LOOKED IN THE MIRROR and didn't find anything beautiful? I think that's because of two things: you were looking for an image the world gave you and told you was beautiful, and you've limited the definition of your beauty to the world's standard.

The world's definition of beauty is kind of a trick. It sets an unrealistic standard designed to provoke comparison and competition. It makes you think you always need more or less of something to meet the standard. Plus, the images we see online aren't always even real! If you hold too tightly to the world's standards of beauty, you will never feel beautiful. It's set up to make you feel *less than*, which wasn't God's design.

When God created you, He created a masterpiece not meant to be compared to any other creation. The image of beauty you were designed to reach is in front of you. You are beautiful because you were created in the image of God. You are beautiful because you're the only one who has what you have to rock. Who you were made to be is more than enough.

Now, go look in the mirror. Take off any worldly lens that has affected the way you see yourself—a lens of insecurity, jealousy, comparison, negativity, self-hatred, or anything else. And stare at yourself.

You are altogether beautiful, my darling.
Wow, the Lord takes such great delight in you.

Look at the color of your eyes, the strands of your hair, and the features of your face. God made you, and you are exactly how He intended you to be. You do not have to "fix" anything or "work" to be anything. You are already beautiful. He created you to reveal a new image of beauty and another side of Himself to the world.

From this day forward, choose to turn your eyes away from the standard of what is "supposed" to make you feel confident and beautiful, and fix your eyes on the One who gives you everything you need to walk into the purpose He has planned for you.

Lord, open my eyes to see myself the
way You see me. And teach me not to be
afraid to believe that I am both beautiful
and beautifully made by You. Amen.

18

People Are Fickle

Jesus Christ is the same yesterday and today and forever.

HEBREWS 13:8

DURING MY SEASON ON *DANCING WITH THE Stars*, I found myself on a journey that I never would have dreamed of going on. Have you ever found yourself doing something you never dreamed you'd be doing? Okay, good. We can relate!

I remember the first night of the competition so clearly. I'd been thrown, physically and mentally, into a dance where I had to hang on to just about everything—my faith, my confidence, the fact that I had rehearsed the moves over and over, and especially my partner—to get through it. When the dance was over, I hung on to favorable remarks from the judges, the comments people made about the performance, and the articles and reviews I read. Why wouldn't I have done that? Everything was so positive! The reviews and comments were *amazing*.

And they lasted exactly one week.

When week two rolled around, I still had a great partner

and the never-ending support of my family and friends, but the judges and the general public weren't nearly as impressed with the second dance. Suddenly, I went from great to mediocre. That quick turn of events taught me one of the most valuable lessons of my life: I could not let what other people thought or said about me affect what I thought and said about myself. Neither the good nor the bad. I learned three words that stung at first but then drove me to a place of faith in God I had never known before: *people are fickle*.

People change. Their comments and opinions change. One day they can think you are the most awesome person on earth, but the next day, they think you're a worm. Yep. People are fickle. There's only one person who has ever lived who does not change, ever: *Jesus*. If you want someone in your life you can always depend on, He's the One.

Stop relying on other people for your sense of value, and stop letting their opinions determine what you think about yourself. Only God can tell you who you really are—*His*.

———————

Father, I want to focus on who You say I am. I take every word the world has said about me and cover it with who You say I am. Thank You for always supporting me— yesterday, today, and forever. Amen.

19

Not a Copy

God created human beings in his own image. In the image of
God he created them; male and female he created them.

GENESIS 1:27 NLT

THE WORD *ORIGINAL* MEANS MUCH MORE TO
me now than it did when I wrote *Live Original.* It has become a
part of almost everything I do. With so many people all searching
for identity, we need to be reminded that we are all created in
the image of God. We are His original masterpieces. So I really
want you to understand what the word *original* means and how
it applies to comparison.

> original (adjective): 1. Present or existing from the beginning;
> first or earliest. 2. Created directly and personally by a parti-
> cular artist; not a copy.[1]

Do you see the end of the second definition? You're not a
copy. So let me ask you this: What is it that drives us to compare ourselves with others? Yep, it's usually the desire to copy or

imitate someone—someone we think is prettier, smarter, more athletic, more popular, or more pulled together. We are created to live in community with other people and to bless one another. But we can end up cursing one another because we are busy comparing instead of celebrating the good in one another. That's not God's plan.

God designed and crafted each of us with amazing individuality. God saw no need to compare one of us with another one, because . . .

You are one of a kind.
There's no one else on earth like you.
There is something of the image of God in you.

Comparison is a tool of the Enemy; it's not of God. What's good about another person is not a threat to you; it's something you can use to build that person up. So the next time you feel tempted to compare yourself to someone else, tell yourself that both of you are valued and needed—*because you are!* And God has a purpose for both of you.

Lord, forgive me for the times I question the way You made me. Help me to see Your workmanship not only in myself but in others. Amen.

20

As Real as It Gets

See what great love the Father has lavished on us, that we
should be called children of God! And that is what we are!

1 JOHN 3:1

NOT LONG AGO I WENT AROUND TO SEVERAL
sororities on a bunch of different college campuses and asked
this question: *What are the people around you struggling with
the most?* No matter where I went, I got pretty much the same
answers: perfectionism, mental illness, depression, anxiety, feelings of loneliness, body image issues, and eating disorders.

These are some huge issues, and I wanted to get to the root
of the problem. Why were these same issues popping up again
and again? Now, the answer is the Enemy himself, but what tac-
tics was he using? As I listened to these girls share their struggles,
I couldn't help but notice the things they were consumed with:
popularity and social media.

Too many of us are looking to social media sites like Instagram
to decide who we are, whether or not we're happy, whether or
not we're popular or beautiful, and if our lives have purpose.

That's not good because Instagram gives us an unrealistic view of the world and other people's lives. Photos are edited to look impossibly perfect and do not truly represent who we are. Stories are edited to make everyone's life sound amazing—and so much better than ours. Comparing ourselves to other people's ideas of perfection is just not healthy.

Time magazine put out an article called "Why Instagram Is the Worst Social Media for Mental Health." Studies found that comparison and lack of "likes" can lead to anxiety, depression, and feelings of loneliness.[1] There's even talk of removing the "like" button altogether. Why? Turns out, it's proven to have a direct effect on our mental health. Because we are determining our worth based off of our likes.

Let me say this once and for all: the answers you're looking for—the life you're looking for—are not on Instagram. Real life isn't about photoshopped perfection. Real life is about imperfect people like you and me, coming to a perfect God and allowing Him to tell us who we really are: His beloved children, the ones He made with His own hands, the ones He adores so much that He sent His own Son to die for us. Now, that's as real as it gets.

Holy Lord, teach me who I am. Not who
the world or friends or Instagram says
I am, but who You say I am. Amen.

Happy Birthday!

How precious are your thoughts about me, O God. They cannot be numbered! I can't even count them; they outnumber the grains of sand!

PSALM 139:17–18 NLT

I HAVE A FRIEND WHO DIDN'T WANT TO acknowledge her birthday because she had just walked through some very difficult situations in the past year. It broke my heart. Regardless of what had happened, it was the day she came into the world, and that was worth a celebration. I tried to throw her a party, but she found out and canceled it. She was at a really low point. And the reality is, I know she's not the only one who has felt like their life isn't worth the celebration.

I get it. Things happen. And some of those things are really hard and painful. But let me say that no matter what you've been through or believe about yourself, your birthday is special.

For starters, the gift of life was the first gift you ever received. Most likely, you were celebrated just because you came into the world. Even if people on earth did not celebrate you, I know heaven was celebrating. Remember, God created us because He wanted a relationship with us. Read Psalm 139 if you're doubting that. God knew you before you were formed in your mother's womb. He saw you, and He has always had a plan for you.

Your birthday is a reminder that God gave you life. There was something about His own image that He wanted to create in you and share with the world. Your birthday is the ultimate affirmation of who you are and why your life matters.

Sometimes we can tell if something we believe about ourselves is a lie by asking if the younger version of ourselves would have believed it. Almost every child's favorite day of the year is their birthday. It usually means a party, cake, attention, and gifts! But somewhere along the way, we can allow the Enemy's lies to take away the beauty and celebration of who we are.

Don't let the Enemy steal this celebration of you. When your birthday rolls around, it's time to party! Now, chances are that today isn't your birthday. But that's okay—every day is a chance to thank God for His gift of life. It is a gift not meant to be overlooked. Your life has so much purpose and value.

———————————

Lord, I thank You for not only creating me in Your image but also for keeping me in Your thoughts. You give me so many reasons to celebrate. Amen.

22

Don't Shut Yourself Down

I praise you because I am fearfully and wonderfully made.

PSALM 139:14

DO YOU EVER MAKE A MISTAKE AND SAY TO yourself, "I'm so stupid"? I've gotta say, nothing annoys me more than to hear someone say something so terrible about themselves. Yet many of us do exactly that. Or maybe we look at someone else—someone we think is smarter, more attractive, or more together than we are—and say, "I'll never have what she has."

This kind of negative self-talk is so easy to do. But it's not innocent. It can be dangerous because words are powerful. And believe me, the Enemy knows it. He's tricky and a liar, and he'll try to get us to believe that our words have no power, that they don't affect our thoughts and moods and actions. But they do. I see it in my husband, Christian, when he runs himself down for a mistake. It changes his whole body language. His shoulders slump, and his smile goes away. He's basically bullying himself, and I just can't stand it. If we truly believe our words have the power of life and death, we will be careful about the way we speak not only to others but also to ourselves.

Let me encourage you to start saying truthful and positive things about yourself. Notice I didn't just say *positive*. You can give yourself a positive self-talk all day long but still feel insecure if it isn't authentic. Truthful talk is what will lift your shoulders up and reset the joy on your face. You can even use Bible verses to talk to yourself. Based on Philippians 4:13, you can say, "I can do anything with Christ's help. He strengthens me." That is positive and truthful. Or you can use Jeremiah 29:11 and say, "Things may be a little tough for me right now, but God knows the plans He has for me, and they are good. He is giving me hope and a future!" You get to decide what you say to yourself, and what you say will affect how you feel and what you do. That's why Proverbs 18:21 says, "The tongue has the power of life and death."

Don't let the Enemy shut down God's purpose in your life by shutting you down with your own words. Speak good words—God's words—over yourself and your life.

Lord, when I start to see everything I think is wrong with me, remind me of who I really am—Your own wonderful creation. Amen.

23

But God Says . . .

The word of God is living and powerful, and sharper than any
two-edged sword.

HEBREWS 4:12 NKJV

LET ME WARN YOU: THE WORDS OF GOD
can't do much for you if all you do is scan them quickly and
then check your social media. But if you read them slowly, with
your heart and mind open, as though they are written especially
for you, like they are truth (because they are), and like they really
mean what they say for you personally (because they do), then
they will change your life.

Below you'll see some of the biggest lies the world wants you
to believe, and then after each one I'll immediately share a truth
from the Word that will knock the breath out of that lie.

The *world* says, "You're not valuable. Nobody cares about you."

But *God's Word* says, "Look at the birds of the air; they do
not sow or reap or store away in barns, and yet your heavenly
Father feeds them. Are you not much more valuable than they?"
(Matthew 6:26).

The *world* says, "You don't matter."

But *God's Word* says, "Since you are precious and honored in my sight, and because I love you, I will give people in exchange for you, nations in exchange for your life" (Isaiah 43:4).

The *world* says, "You'll never amount to anything. There's just too much wrong with you!"

But *God's Word* says, "Even before he made the world, God loved us and chose us in Christ to be holy and without fault in his eyes" (Ephesians 1:4 NLT).

The *world* says, "You never do anything right!"

But *God's Word* says, "Now to Him who is able to do far more abundantly beyond all that we ask or think, according to the power that works within us" (Ephesians 3:20 NASB).

Wherever you are right now, speak the words of these verses. Say what God says. And don't sit there and just awkwardly mumble them—claim them! These words will keep you grounded in how God thinks about you for the rest of your life. Keep them on your mind and in your heart, return to them often, memorize them, think about them, and let them become the foundation of who you believe you are.

———————

Lord, as I read and study Your Word, I pray that You would show me who I really am and who You want me to be. Amen.

Get the Ugly Out!

Give all your worries and cares to God, for he cares about you.

1 PETER 5:7 NLT

HAVE YOU EVER HAD A TIME IN YOUR LIFE when you just felt ugly? Maybe it was because you had a break-out or you got a bad haircut or that outfit you thought would look so good on you didn't really look good at all.

Once, when I was in high school, I got the worst haircut ever. My basketball team was scheduled to start a tournament the next day, and I didn't like the way my hair fell in my eyes as I ran up and down the court. I thought I *had* to have a trim, but my hairdresser couldn't do it. So I went to the salon in a big discount store and thought, *How bad could it be?*

It was bad.

The girl took off an inch of hair on one side and four inches on the other! It looked horrible, and I literally cried whenever I looked in the mirror. Not dramatic at all, right? I've had plenty of other experiences that made me feel ugly on the outside, and perhaps you have too. But what I really want to talk about is a different kind of ugly—the kind you feel on the inside. I'm talking about fear, anger, resentment, jealousy—all those negative emotions that cause you to think you're weak, unimportant, and, yes, ugly.

When you feel ugly on the outside, you can clear up the breakout, let your hair grow, or change your outfit. When you feel ugly on the inside, though, none of those strategies will work. When the problem is on the inside, the solution has to start on the inside too—by letting go of the fear, shame, guilt, jealousy, disappointment, anger, and all the other things that make you feel ugly and unworthy.

Is something making you feel ugly on the inside? Release all that pain and roll it over to God—and let Him free you so you can feel truly beautiful inside.

———————————

Lord, I come to You with all this ugly mess that's stuck inside me, and I lay it all at Your feet. Wash it away. Wash me clean so that I can feel like Your beautiful child again. Amen.

25

Cool and Confident

For we are God's masterpiece. He has created us anew in Christ Jesus, so we can do the good things he planned for us long ago.

EPHESIANS 2:10 NLT

I USED TO COMPARE MYSELF TO EVERYONE around me. I wanted to make sure my clothes were like theirs and our makeup looked similar and our legs were the same size. And I will tell you, if you don't already know, that is exhausting and impossible to keep up. Because as soon as you start to compare yourself to others, you position yourself to feel "less than" them and less about who you are.

God made each of us unique. That's cool to me and very freeing. Take a look around—no one is just like you! Cherish what makes you different from every other person in the world. Cool is not a certain look, a way of acting, liking the "right" things, or disliking the things other people say aren't cool. It's being confident in what you're doing and in who you are.

Here's my challenge:

Stop comparing your legs to the person beside you, and just compare your left to your right and use them to their best potential. Stop waiting to see what all your friends are wearing, and just wear what you love because you love it! Stop making sure your makeup is on trend, and just do it the way that makes you feel confident. And if you don't like to wear makeup, then don't. When you become confident, you become cool with who you are. And when you're cool with who you are, you won't be tempted to compare yourself to anyone around you.

I once dyed my hair pink, and so many people said, "I've always wanted to do that but didn't have the confidence." They were saying their confidence was tied to their appearance. Our confidence must be rooted in something deeper—in God—so that we can freely live as our unique and original selves.

Being who you are as a child of God is a miracle, and it comes with miraculous power through the help of the Holy Spirit. It doesn't come through pink hair, good eyebrows, or the perfect body. *It comes through the Holy Spirit.* Be cool and confident in who God has created you to be, and live the life God has called you to live.

Holy Father, it's so easy to look around and compare myself to others—and then to see myself as less-than. Help me remember that I can be confident because I was created by You. Amen.

26

Born to Be Royal

You are a chosen people, a royal priesthood, a holy nation, God's special possession, that you may declare the praises of him who called you out of darkness into his wonderful light.

1 PETER 2:9

I ONCE SPOKE AT AN EVENT WHERE ALL THE girls were asked to write about who they thought they were. Everyone had a sheet of paper that said, "I am _____," and they were to fill in the blank. I noticed that all the girls were using some pretty negative adjectives to describe their identities.

I've heard many people say they believe they're worthless. That is a scary lie because believing it never leads to anything good. Feelings of worthlessness creep in when we think we can't fulfill what is being asked of us.

A scene from *The Princess Diaries* captures this perfectly. Princess Mia feels completely overwhelmed and wants to give up, but her security guard, Joe, says, "No one can quit being who they really are, not even a princess. You can refuse the job, but you are a princess by birth."

Princess Mia responds, "How can I tell if I can even do the job?" And Joe replies, "By simply, simply trying."[1]

Many times, we want to be sure we can do something before we even try. We hesitate because we feel like we aren't good enough or pretty enough or strong enough. Princess Mia didn't think she could ever measure up to the role she was born into. But if you've seen the movie, you know that she could. And in the end, it was not about how she felt or what she had to offer. Instead, it was simply about who she was. She was royalty because of who her father was. Just like you.

How do you fill in the blanks about yourself? Are the adjectives all negative? Have you ever said to yourself, "I can't do this" or "I won't get this right" or "This is too much for me"? Maybe you need to hear what Mia heard and eventually came to believe: you're royalty. Not because of what you can do. But because that's who you were born to be.

God, some days it's a lot easier to believe the lies than it is to believe the truth. Help me to believe what You say about me—that I'm chosen by You. Amen.

27

Not Your Two-Mama's Two-Step

Anyone who belongs to Christ has become a new person.
The old life is gone; a new life has begun!

2 CORINTHIANS 5:17 NLT

WHEN I WAS IN MIDDLE SCHOOL, THE TWO-step was a hip-hop dance spun off of a popular rap song. To other people, especially those beyond their teenage years, it's an old country dance. I once told my mom's mom—I call her Two-Mama—that I knew how to do the two-step, and she said, "We used to do that back in my day!" I was shocked because the two-step I was talking about seemed like a weird dance for a grandma to do. I started doing today's version of the two-step for her, and she quickly realized it was not the two-step she learned. It just had the same name.

Something similar often happens to each of us. Like the two-step, our names might stay the same, but if we aren't careful, we can stray far away from our true selves, from who God created us to be. And it can happen so easily. Because the things in this world change quickly, and without even realizing it, we can change with them. Sure, my name has always been Sadie, but there were times when I just went along with the crowd. Before I realized it, I was listening to music I thought I'd never listen to, watching shows that I couldn't even sit through now, and dating the guys I knew I shouldn't date.

Your identity is one of the most foundational pieces of your life. So it's important for me to ask this question, and it's even more important for you to answer it: Who are you? I'm not talking about what you like to do in your free time or your Enneagram number. I mean, who are you, really, at your core? Has the dance of your life changed into something you don't even recognize?

As you think about those questions, remember where your true identity comes from: God. He's the One who created you, and He's the only One who can define you. So what does God have to say about who you are? You are a chosen (1 Peter 2:9) and beloved (John 3:16) child of God (1 John 3:1). And that's a truth you can two-step to!

———————

Father, I know that my confidence, my
freedom, and my faith come only from You.
Show me the ways I've drifted away from You,
and draw me back to Your side. Amen.

28

So Far from Worthless

For you created my inmost being; you knit me together in my mother's womb.

PSALM 139:13

IN LIFE YOU'LL FACE ALL KINDS OF SITUATIONS where the world will try to tell you who you are. People may say that you're not very smart, you're awkward, you "have issues," your dreams will never come true, you're extra, or you're worth nothing because of where you came from, who your parents are, the house you live in, the color of your skin, or where you buy your clothes. I beg you: don't let the world tell you who you are. Only God can truly define you.

Dig into His Word and find out who you truly are. You are a child of the King of the universe. You don't have to be over-whelmed by anything or intimidated by anyone. You're God's son or daughter, which means you can do whatever He calls you to do. All you have to do is try, and He will do the rest.

I know that a lot of young people do feel worthless, though, so I want to address it a bit more. What I believe tends to happen is that you replay the hard conversations you've had and the most painful moments you've been through, the ones that caused shame to rise up in you. Then you let those fruitless thoughts lead you to believe that you are worthless. Read this and take it personally:

You are far from worthless.

It's time to reject the lies of the Enemy and embrace the truth that the King of the universe created you. That makes you—yes, *you*—a child of the King. That's your worth. That's what you have always been. Don't let this world or anyone in it tell you otherwise. *Believe* you are who God says you are, and then go out and *live* like you are who God says you are.

———————

Lord, show me through Your Word who I really am. And then help me to teach others who they are in You too. Amen.

29

Are You Riding the Crazy Train?

"The truth will set you free."

JOHN 8:32

ONE NIGHT MY FRIEND BRIGHTON AND I were sitting around talking and laughing, just having fun like girls do. Before we knew it, we'd come up with a concept that describes the life cycle of fear that the whole world seemed to be on. We called it the "crazy train." We started by asking a series of questions we thought teenage girls could relate to, mostly about guys and relationship stuff.

For example:

- Have you ever looked over your boyfriend's shoulder to see who he was texting?
- Have you ever seen a group text that you weren't a part of and asked, *Why didn't they include me? Maybe they don't they like me anymore.*

- Have you ever driven over to your boyfriend's house because he didn't answer any of your calls or texts?

The crazy train is a series of thoughts that moves you in a specific direction—not necessarily a good one—and you just keep riding it, never entertaining the idea that you could take your life in a different direction if you'd simply change the way you think.

I once heard Alex Seeley, pastor of The Belonging Co in Nashville, Tennessee, say that when Satan lies to us, he often does it through our own thoughts. He'll plant a thought in our minds—a lie—and the next thing we know, we believe it! The moment we agree with that lie is the moment we give the Enemy power in our lives. Believing the first lie only makes it easier for him to convince us of the second one and third one—and then it's "welcome to the crazy train!" And the longer you stay on the train, the crazier things will get, and there's a good chance the whole situation will become really ugly before it's over.

Be honest with yourself right now. Are you taking a ride on the crazy train? What lies are you believing? Search out God's truth instead. Trust me: everything in your life would be so much better if you'd just take the leap and jump off the crazy train.

―――――――

Lord, show me the truth of what I'm believing. If there are lies in my life, expose them and fill me with the truth of Your Word instead. Amen.

30

Friends Don't Let Friends Ride the Crazy Train

Encourage one another and build each other up.

1 THESSALONIANS 5:11

WHEN SOMEONE IN YOUR LIFE IS LETTING their feelings spin out of control and causing them to think, act, and speak in ways that aren't good for them—aka when they're on a crazy train—you can be the person who stands in the middle of the track and yells, "Jump off! Jump off! That train is crazy!"

It takes some maturity to help someone off the crazy train, though. If a friend is jumping to conclusions about a group of girls looking at her, you might find it easier to join her negativity and say, "You're right; those girls probably were talking about you" than to say, "I don't know what they were talking about, but if it was about you, it had to be good!" If a friend is insecure about her boyfriend, you might find it easier to go along with her assumptions and say, "Yeah, I'll bet your boyfriend *is* cheating on you," than to say, "He's never done anything to make you think you can't trust him." (Of course, that's if you know his character. We don't want to encourage friends to ignore red flags.)

Instead of making a situation worse for someone, you can be the person who makes it better. When your friend starts moving down the crazy-train track, you can say, "Okay, let's stop. We don't know all the details or the context of what you saw, so let's not jump to conclusions." In those moments, you have the opportunity to stop the crazy train and to bring wisdom and peace to your friend who is in the middle of juggling a lot of emotions.

A good friend is one who says what God says. When someone you care about is overwhelmed with negative emotions such as fear, anxiety, anger, or hurt, overwhelm them with the transforming Word of God. Remind them that God says they have a hope and a future (Jeremiah 29:11), that He loves them with an everlasting love that will never turn on them or fade away (Jeremiah 31:3), that He's always there when they call to Him (Psalm 55:16), and that He will never, ever, ever fail them or forsake them (Deuteronomy 31:6).

Lord, teach me to be the kind of friend who sees when a friend is believing lies and acting in harmful ways. And please give me the courage to reach out to them with Your truth. Amen.

31

Sharks and Dolphins

The LORD is my rock, my fortress and my deliverer.

2 SAMUEL 22:2

WHEN I READ 2 SAMUEL 22:2, I'M NOT GOING to lie, my mind goes to sharks and dolphins. You may think that's strange, and well, it is. But my mind is just like that.

I've read news stories about sharks trying to attack someone and dolphins swimming up to surround the potential victim, keeping that person safe and maybe even saving his or her life. It's like the dolphins form a fortress around the person, delivering them from injury or death.

My friend Laney is like that. I tell her all the time that she reminds me of a dolphin. When fear tries to attack someone, she has this amazing ability to surround that person with the truth of God's Word. She uses the Word to build a fortress around the person that fear can't get through. She's done that for me many times.

Once, when I was about to go on tour, I had a full-on panic attack. I was sitting in the hallway crying and saying, "I cannot do this."

Next thing I know, Laney was flying down the hallway saying, "No, no, no, no, no." She looked like an angry mom pointing her finger, as she went on to say, "You do not get to do this. You do not get to quit because of fear. God has done too much in you." It is so good to have a friend to remind you of truth. To say, "God has not given us a spirit of fear, but of power and of love and of a sound mind," which is truth pulled from 2 Timothy 1:7 (NKJV).

I love that Laney does this for me. Christian is great at it too. But neither Laney nor my husband can be there every time fear sneaks up. So I've learned to fight fear using the Word on my own, with the help of the One who gives peace: Jesus. Let me encourage you to learn to do that too—just speak the Word to yourself and ask God to help it work on your mind and emotions.

Don't stop there, though. Challenge yourself to become the kind of friend that Laney is to me. Be the one who speaks the Word over those who are afraid and who helps them use it to push back their fears.

———————

God, when I feel fear sneaking up on me, remind me to call out to You and speak the truth of Your Word. Help me to be a dolphin—a defender— when those I love are under attack. Amen.

32

Ice Cold or Red Hot?

"You will seek me and find me when you seek me with all your heart."

JEREMIAH 29:13

WHEN MY FRIENDS AND I WERE LITTLE, WE used to play this game called Red Hot. You probably played it too. It's where you hide something and another person tries to find it. If the seeker is far away from the hidden object, you say, "You're ice cold." If they move even farther away, you say, "You're getting colder." But if they move closer, you say, "You're getting warmer." Then, when they're practically right on top of it, you say, "Oh, you're hot! You're on fire!"

Sometimes I look around—at restaurants, in malls and coffee shops, anywhere people are gathered—and I see people mindlessly scrolling through their phones. Maybe it's Instagram or Snapchat or TikTok. Whatever it is, they're just scrolling and scrolling; following and following; liking, liking, and liking. And I think to myself, *I wonder if they're finding what they're looking for.*

I once asked my Instagram followers what they're searching

for in life, and the top answers were peace, love, confidence, joy, and purpose. I then looked up the average time people spend scrolling through social media just searching. I suddenly realized we are ice cold. We are scrolling and aimlessly searching, all while we're desperate to find true meaning. But we are searching in the wrong place.

Because the things we're searching for in this life—the important things, like love and peace and purpose—aren't found on our phones. They are found in the Word of God. If we would put down our phone sometimes and pick up the Word, that's when we would be "red hot and on fire." God's Word is the source of everything we're searching for because it's the voice of God speaking into our lives.

There's a promise in God's Word: seek and you will find. So if you're looking for love? Find it in God. Looking for peace? Find it in God. Looking for hope? Find it—you guessed it—in God. When we decide to follow God, He pours His Holy Spirit into our lives. And with His Spirit comes all the fruit of the Spirit: "love, joy, peace, patience, kindness, goodness, faithfulness, gentleness, and self-control" (Galatians 5:22–23 NLT).

So stop scrolling and find everything you're searching for in the Word.

———————

Holy Father, I'm searching for You and Your presence in my life. Show Yourself to me and lead me to Your purpose for my life. Amen.

33

The Handbook for Life

This world is fading away, along with everything that people crave. But anyone who does what pleases God will live forever.

1 JOHN 2:17 NLT

I OFTEN THINK MANY OF US ARE FOLLOWING the same handbook for life. No one has a copy of it, but we know exactly what it says. It's an unwritten set of guidelines about how to thrive and be successful in life, and its author is "The World." It goes something like this:

"Look out for number one."

"You do you, boo."

"You only live once."

"Whatever it takes to get likes."

I have to ask: Is anyone happy doing what that handbook says? Does anyone actually *like* the outcomes they're getting?

Even though the world in Paul's day was different than ours, the problem was the same. He wrote this passage to the church in Rome:

Do not be conformed to this world [any longer with its superficial values and customs], but be transformed and progressively changed [as you mature spiritually] by the renewing of your mind [focusing on godly values and ethical attitudes], so that you may prove [for yourselves] what the will of God is, that which is good and acceptable and perfect [in His plan and purpose for you]. (Romans 12:2 AMP)

Wow. These words will give you life and set you free. Paul told us exactly how to live. He said we are not to be "conformed to this world," which goes much further than simply saying, "Don't pay attention to it." He understood how hard the world works to influence us and said, "Don't let that happen." Why? Because when you look below the surface of the world's superficial values—our social media presence, money, fame, or popularity—you'll find nothing of lasting value. For the path to life and true fulfillment, we have to set our minds on things that last.

Don't let this world toss you up and down with every new trend and idea. Instead, place your confidence in God and His never-changing love by digging deep into His Word—the real Handbook for life.

─────────────

Lord, when this world sets out to change me, I pray that You would be a shield around me and keep me close to You. Amen.

34

Get to Know His Voice

We live by faith, not by sight.

2 CORINTHIANS 5:7

I ABSOLUTELY LOVE THE STORY OF JESUS walking out to His disciples on the water (Matthew 14:22–33). There's just so much truth in those few lines. One of the things that really convicts me is that everyone in that boat saw the same thing. It was nighttime for everyone, it was windy for everyone, and the waves were big for everyone. But only one of them walked out on the water to meet Jesus. Why was it different for Peter that night?

I think it has to do with Peter's words right after Jesus said, "Don't be afraid." Peter said, "Lord, if it's you, . . . tell me to come to you on the water" (vv. 27–28).

That statement is so powerful to me, and here's why: If I had been on that boat, seeing something blurry out there and wondering if it were Jesus, I feel like I would have said, "Hey, Jesus, come a little closer so I can make sure it's really You. If I see that it's You, *then* I'll walk out to You." But Peter didn't say that. Peter knew that if he heard Jesus' voice, he was stepping out. The Lord was inviting Peter into a moment with Him, and he didn't want to miss it.

How many moments do we miss with Jesus because we're afraid to step out of the boat? Because we want to see ahead of time how it's all going to work out? Because we don't know—or fully trust—His voice?

Peter stepped out of the boat because He knew Jesus' voice. If we want to be bold in our faith, we have to know His voice too. We have to know His Word. The fact is, if we want to follow Jesus, we have to trust the Word. In order to trust it, we need to have confidence in it, and in order to have confidence, we have to know it.

Let's be honest: the unknown makes us uncomfortable. So we ask Jesus to just come a little closer and to prove Himself before we step out to meet Him. But He has already given us His Word to be a lamp to our feet (Psalm 119:105) and to guide us when the wind is blowing and the waves are crashing and we can't clearly see where we're going.

Don't miss another invitation from Jesus. Open up His Word, get to know His voice, and step out of the boat.

Lord, give me the desire to learn
more from Your Word. Teach me to know
and follow Your voice. Amen.

35

Disgusted with Fear

Behold, God is my salvation, I will trust and not be afraid; "For YAH, the LORD, is my strength and song; He also has become my salvation."

ISAIAH 12:2 NKJV

FEAR HAS ALWAYS BEEN AN ISSUE FOR ME, but during my teenage years, the struggle was really intense. When I say *intense*, I mean that every morning I woke up afraid of something. Every night I went to bed anxious. And throughout each day I was fearful. I lived my *whole life* in fear—and that's not an exaggeration.

I knew that the Bible says, "Do not fear" many times. And I knew that was great advice—after all, God said it. But I simply couldn't shake the fear. If you've struggled with fear, you know how hard it is when someone just tells you, "Don't be afraid." It is a lot easier to say than to do.

I finally became completely disgusted with the way fear was controlling my life. I began praying intensely—every night—asking God to set me free from the power of fear. And each night I gained a little more strength and released a little more fear. There was no sudden breakthrough, but over time I gained a new level of confidence and courage.

As I prayed, the Holy Spirit began to show me that I needed to change the way I was praying. Instead of asking God to change my situation, I needed to ask Him to change my heart. A lot of times when we struggle with something, our prayer life becomes simply a plea for God to change our situation. But sometimes we're in that situation for a reason. And rather than God getting us out of it, we need Him to meet us in it. It's only when we stop praying for God to change our circumstances and start asking Him to change our hearts that we experience the peace that passes understanding (Philippians 4:7).

Are you letting fear run rampant in your life? Is it keeping you from stepping into His plans for you? Have you reached the place where you're disgusted with fear and ready to deal with it? Cry out to God. Ask Him to change your heart and to meet you where you are.

———————

Lord, help me to reach the point where I hate fear and what it does to me—enough to really deal with it. Change my heart so that my confidence is in You. Amen.

36

From Fear to Favorite

When I am afraid, I will put my trust in you. I praise God for what he has promised. I trust in God, so why should I be afraid?

PSALM 56:3–4 NLT

I ONCE SPOKE AT AN EVENT WITH OLYMPIC gymnasts. During the Q&A portion, a little girl asked the gymnasts, "What's the scariest thing you've ever done in gymnastics?"

I couldn't wait to hear their answers, because although I'm not a gymnast, I love watching them on TV.

I was fascinated by the gymnasts' responses. Each told a story about a scary move, and several said they were frightened of those particular moves because they'd been hurt doing them before. They didn't want to sprain another ankle, do another face-plant, or end up in a pile underneath the high bar.

What really caught my attention was that they all made essentially the same statement in the end: the element they were most afraid of became their favorite. Why? Because they chose to face the thing that frightened them. They kept practicing until they mastered the move and were no longer afraid.

They came to love what they once hated—all because they faced their fears head-on and conquered them.

Here's the thing: Satan is afraid of you becoming everything God wants you to be, and he tries to make you afraid of it too. It's not a coincidence that you just happen to be scared of the very thing God has given you the ability to do. If you can identify what the Enemy wants you to fear, then that's most likely connected to your purpose. And it's the *very thing* you need to go after with faith.

Ask yourself, What scares you more than anything else? And I don't mean spiders, snakes, or sharks. I am talking about things like the message you have to share, the people you want to reach, the place you need to go, and that thing you know you need to do. Now, go face it! That's right—face it.

I'm pretty sure the Olympic gymnasts would join me in encouraging you to take a deep breath and jump into the thing you fear most. You are not alone. Every person you see out there fulfilling their purpose had to just jump in. They've done it. I've done it. And you can too! Trust God. Because once you do, it will be so great that you'll wonder why you waited so long.

———————

Lord Jesus, show me Your love in the midst
of my biggest fears, and give me the courage
to risk doing what I am afraid of. Amen.

37

Who's Talking?

Trust in the LORD with all your heart; do not depend on your own understanding.

PROVERBS 3:5 NLT

WHEN I RECEIVED THE PHONE CALL LETTING me know that *Dancing with the Stars* wanted me on their show, I was hit with a big fear moment. Honestly, I had a meltdown—and it was major. I went to bed that night scared, and when I woke up, I was still scared. I knew this would be an amazing opportunity and experience, but I couldn't find a way to slide out of the grip of fear. Besides the fact that I had never really danced in front of anyone—not that kind of formal dancing—I was going to have to leave Louisiana in my junior year of high school and move to Los Angeles to compete in front of millions of people. This was no small yes.

That day, I took my little sister, Bella, out to lunch. As I told her about the call and my hesitations, she stopped me and looked me right in the eye. "Sadie, can I ask you a question?" she said in her eleven-year-old, matter-of-fact way. "Is this the fear talking, or is this Sadie talking?"

Y'all, I was pretty shook in that moment, I'm not going to lie. I'd just gotten called out by an eleven-year-old!

Who *was* talking? Was it the fear, or was it me? Bella could have simply said, "Sadie, this is fear talking." But she made her point in the form of a question, knowing I'd have to wrestle with the answer and that it would be good for me. Of course it was the fear talking. I didn't want to admit it, but what was I going to do? I couldn't sit there and set an example for her that fear is a legit excuse to say no to whatever doors God opens for you. I don't believe that at all! Her question was all I needed to drop my excuse and pick up the faith to say yes.

So here's a question for you: Are you torn right now because you really want to do something but you're afraid? Ask yourself the same question Bella asked me: "[Say your name here], is this fear talking, or is this you talking?"

I challenge you to say yes to whatever you are currently saying no to. Don't let fear make you say no when God is leading you to say yes.

———————————

Lord, give me the strength to say yes when
You want me to do something. Give me guidance
to know what to do next in my life. Amen.

38

Go Away, Fear!

The Spirit God gave us does not make us timid, but gives us power, love and self-discipline.

2 TIMOTHY 1:7

YOU'VE PROBABLY HEARD THAT A LOT OF people struggle with the fear of public speaking. That's been true for me. If you've heard me speak in a large arena or on YouTube, where the whole world can watch, you may be thinking, *No way!* (If you have, thanks for being there!) I had to learn to face my fears every time I stepped on a stage or in front of a camera.

Though I truly believe I am now living fearlessly, I'll confess that sometimes I still get a little nervous when I speak in front of lots of people. But it's an excited-nervous instead of a scared-nervous. I used to allow anxiety to keep me from wanting to speak. Now I can hardly wait to get in front of the audience because of the confidence the Lord has built up in me.

I know this is going to sound funny, but one thing that helped me overcome my fear was "speaking" to my fear. When I would get overly anxious for no reason, I would literally say out loud, "Nope! In the name of Jesus, go away, fear." The way I have learned to speak to fear reminds me of my dog named Cabo. She will bark and bark and bark, and the more I ignore her, the longer she will keep barking. But when I acknowledge she is there and tell her to stop, she usually does. The longer I ignored fear, the more it bothered me. But when I started acknowledging it and standing up to it, then it started to go away.

The key ingredient to overcoming fear is not just speaking to it; it's speaking to it in Jesus' name. When I tell fear to go away and leave me alone in the name of Jesus, I say it with lots of force and a little bit of sass. That short speech has become my anthem. I don't care if I sound a little silly saying it. It works!

The next time you find yourself nose-to-nose with something that scares you—whether it's public speaking, ending a not-so-good-for-you relationship, or starting over someplace new—stand up to that fear. Give it a little straight talk, and tell it to leave you alone in Jesus' name.

Lord, You know the fears that plague me, but today I name them and lay them at your feet. And in Your name, I say, "Go away, fear!" Amen.

39

On the Other Side

Say to those with fearful hearts, "Be strong, and do not fear, for your God is coming to destroy your enemies. He is coming to save you."

ISAIAH 35:4 NLT

HOW MANY THOUGHTS OF FEAR CONSUME your mind? On a scale of one to ten, with ten being off-the-charts high, how fearful would you say you are?

When you're afraid and struggling to face your fears, it's vital to trust God *while you're still afraid*. You see, your peace is often waiting for you on the other side of trust. I've had a lot of experiences where God met me once I stared down my fear, pushed through it, and did what I needed to do.

When we're afraid, we tend to pray and ask God for peace *before* we'll step out and do what frightens us. But most of the time, we need to simply *move forward*. Once we break through the fear, God gives us the most amazing sense of peace—but it doesn't always come while we're still deciding whether to conquer it or not.

If you're waiting for a sense of peace to come so you can deal with your fear, you could be waiting a long time. If you will be brave and march straight into that fearful situation, having faith that God will bring you through it, that's probably where you'll find the peace you're looking for.

The first step is to name your fears. Why? Because in order to move beyond fear, you have to know what you're afraid of. Only then can you face those fears and trust God to see you through to the other side.

Here's the amazing part: once you get to the other side of fear, once you've had that breakthrough you need, you'll look back on the things you were once afraid of and ask yourself, *Why was I so scared of that?* And that's the power of God in your life.

So let me ask you this: What are you afraid of?

———————————

Lord, help me to name the things that
frighten me, and show me how You are bigger
and greater than they are. I will trust
You to help me face my fears. Amen.

40

Facing Lions

I prayed to the Lord, and he answered me. He freed me from all my fears.

PSALM 34:4 NLT

THE STORY OF DANIEL IS ONE OF MY favorites because he truly *was* rooted in God. I also like his story because of what happened in Daniel 6.

At the beginning of the chapter, we learn King Darius put Daniel in a position of leadership over the entire kingdom (vv. 1-3). The other leaders didn't like that, and they plotted against Daniel (vv. 4-5). They went to the king and suggested that he decree that everyone pray to him alone or risk being thrown into a den of hungry lions. The men knew Daniel would never pray to King Darius, because he was devoted to the God of Israel. They knew it so well that they asked the king to put his decree in writing so it could not be changed (vv. 8-9).

As soon as Daniel heard about the decree, he had an anxiety attack. His mouth went dry. His knees went weak. Cue the dramatic music because he could not handle it, right? Wrong!

Daniel went to his room and prayed to the Lord with the windows open—where everyone could hear him (v. 10). Then, in short, the men told the king about it, and Daniel was tossed in a lions' den.

God could have saved Daniel immediately, but that wasn't what He had in mind. God chose to send an angel to shut the lions' mouths. Notice that all Daniel did was trust God, and God sent an angel to do the rest. You may be fighting and clawing some lions in your life, trying to silence them yourself when you really only need to be still and allow God to send an angel to shut their mouths.

For me, the lions represent fear. Your lions might be people's rude opinions, conflicts in friendships, unhealthy relationships, natural disasters, sicknesses, or unexpected life changes. Lions are a part of life. It is important, though, to face your lions with faith. Stop believing in the power of the lions and believe instead in the power of God.

———————

Holy Father, when the lions in my life start roaring, I ask You—by Your power—to hush them up and help me hear only You. Amen.

41

F.E.A.R.

Don't be deceived, my dear brothers and sisters.

JAMES 1:16

THERE'S AN OLD ACRONYM FOR FEAR THAT I've found helpful to remember: *False Evidence Appearing Real.* You see, one of the main reasons people become afraid is that they see, hear, or experience something that serves as evidence that something is real when it's not. The Enemy knows that once you believe something is real, it's real to you. But no matter what *appears* to be real, what is more real—the most real of all—is God and His Word.

Here's the thing, though. Sometimes false evidence really does appear real, even to experts. Let me give you an example: One day, Two-Mama (that's what I call my mom's mom) noticed a dark, round spot on my foot. I immediately became worried. I asked a family friend who is a doctor about it, and he suggested I get it checked out. I showed it to another doctor friend, who said it looked like a blue nevus—a kind of deep-skin mole—or perhaps some type of skin cancer, and that I should see a dermatologist. That really got my anxiety up!

The dermatologist said it definitely looked like a blue nevus. I thought for sure I had skin cancer, and I had every reason to think so because even the doctor said it. At that point, I was almost paralyzed with fear. When the dermatologist began scraping the spot for the biopsy, it started fading and almost disappeared.

Y'all, it was not a blue nevus. It was an ink spot from some T-shirt dye I had made the week before and had completely forgotten about. The dye was strong, so the spot hadn't come off even after days of soap and water.

Three doctors looked at that spot and said it looked like a blue nevus, which threw me into a major fear crisis. In reality, I never had anything to fear at all. Fear is like my blue-nevus-that-wasn't—false evidence appearing real. Big time. When we start thinking false evidence represents something real, and we let fear explode in our hearts and minds, we're headed in a dangerous direction.

When you're afraid, turn to God. Ask Him to show you what is real—and what is just F.E.A.R.

Lord, I pray that You give me the wisdom
to know what is real and true, and
what is a lie of the Enemy. Amen.

42

When the Evidence Is Real

The LORD your God is the one who goes with you to fight for you against your enemies to give you victory.

DEUTERONOMY 20:4

SOMETIMES THE ENEMY TRAPS US INTO thinking that false evidence is real—that bad things are happening when they really aren't, like with my blue-nevus-that-wasn't (page 86).

But what if it had been something bad? People are diagnosed with skin cancers all the time. People are terminally ill. People lose their jobs. Houses catch on fire. Teenagers become addicted to drugs. People we love pass away. All these things are real. They do happen, and the evidence supporting them is not false at all. It's real.

Gaining victory over fear does not mean that we can only be free from fear when something that seems bad turns out to be okay, like with my not-real blue nevus. It means we can stay brave, bold, confident, and strong in our faith whether a situation is a false alarm or the real thing. The Bible doesn't say, "Do not fear when something you thought would be scary isn't scary after all." It says, "Do not fear." Period. And actually, it's usually God saying, "Do not fear—*for I am with you.*" He doesn't say, "Do not fear—good luck!" God gives you a reason to not be afraid. Because He promises to be with you. And that promise includes when you face truly frightening situations. That's when faith proves itself. That's when you get to show yourself and those around you how strong a person can be in Jesus and in the power of the Holy Spirit. As I've said before, to live fearless does not mean trying to find a way to make things not scary. It means looking the scary things in the eye and staring them down because God is in you and with you, and He is bigger than fear.

You don't have to accept the Enemy's lie and let him intimidate you with false evidence that appears real. And even when you're faced with something real that is genuinely frightening, you don't have to let that fear overwhelm you. You have a choice. Choose to believe God is bigger and that He's got you.

Lord, I declare right now that You are bigger and stronger than any fear or threat I will ever face. And I will trust You to always take care of me. Amen.

43

Journey to Fearlessness

The LORD is my light and my salvation—whom shall I fear? The LORD is the stronghold of my life—of whom shall I be afraid?

PSALM 27:1

DURING MY FIRST WINTER JAM TOUR, I WAS still wrestling with intense fears, but I had committed to releasing those fears to God through equally intense prayer. Though it was only a ten-day tour, I was so afraid of public speaking that I didn't want to be there. I was just doing a Q&A about *Duck Dynasty*—not even sharing a message—but I was so intimidated by the crowd. Each night before I went onstage, the crowd sang "There Is Power in the Name of Jesus." As I shook in fear, waiting to go onstage, I prayed, "I do believe there is power in the name of Jesus. Help me to live like I believe it." And as I prayed, the fear got smaller—or maybe my faith got way bigger. So instead of doing a Q&A that night, I shared a message. And *that* is really where and when I became a speaker.

Then, one night, as I was praying and getting ready to speak in front of about twenty thousand people, our security guard walked up and said, "Sadie, are you okay with going onstage tonight?"

"Yeah. Why not?"

He then told me about a terrorist attack that had happened that day at a concert in another country, on a stage very much like mine. Never doubt that the Enemy is strategic. I could have put the grip of fear back on me that night, but I had decided to trust that faith was greater than fear. Normally, fear would have consumed me, but that night I thought, *Tonight of all nights, I need to share this message. I need to be out there praying for our world.* And that's what I did.

I learned three huge lessons from that experience:

- No matter how afraid you may be right now, you don't have to stay that way.
- No one can deal with your fear except you. It's up to you to make a change.
- Pray. Because you'll never kick fear out of your life on your own. You need God.

The journey to fearlessness wasn't easy for me, and it may not be easy for you. But I can promise you this: it's worth it.

———————

Holy Father, show me the next step I need to take in this journey to fearlessness. I know You will be beside me. Amen.

44

A Fear God Can Use

"Announce to the army, 'Anyone who trembles with fear may turn back and leave Mount Gilead.'" So twenty-two thousand men left, while ten thousand remained.

JUDGES 7:3

I BELIEVE THERE ARE TWO KINDS OF FEAR. One kind says, "Okay, God. I get what You want me to do. And even though this scares me, I'm going to trust You to see me through." That's the kind of fear God can use. The other kind of fear says, "Okay, God. I get what You want me to do. But no way. Uh-uh. I'm out of here." Clearly, that's *not* the kind of fear God will use.

Let me give you an example. Both kinds of fear show up in the story of Gideon in Judges 7. Earlier, God had convinced Gideon (who was not exactly a model of bravery) that he was the man to lead Israel into battle against the Midianites (page 16). So Gideon rounded up thirty-two thousand men. "You have too many men," God said (v. 2). Then the Lord said to tell "anyone who trembles with fear" to go home (v. 3). Twenty-two thousand thought, *Nope. No way. We're out of here*. Isn't it crazy that what disqualified them was fear, yet Gideon himself was afraid? So what was the difference? I believe it was the willingness to be used by God even in the face of fear.

Later, after God again thinned Gideon's army down to only three hundred men, Gideon himself was still afraid. *Three hundred men* against an enemy army that was too big to count! We'd understand if Gideon ran away, right? But he didn't. God stepped in and reassured Gideon by showing him just how afraid the enemy was of him. Gideon then led his men to the battle—a battle God had already won for them (7:9–8:28).

Do you see the two different kinds of fear? Twenty-two thousand men gave in to their fear. They missed out on the victory that was waiting for them because they were unwilling to face that fear. But Gideon entrusted his fears to God, and God was able to work with his fears and show him a miraculous victory.

The Lord doesn't fault us for having fears. In fact, He's more than willing to work with our fears and lead us to the victory that's waiting on the other side of them. The real question then is this: Are we—and our fears—willing to work with God?

Holy Father, You know all the fears of my heart. I give You those fears and trust that You will work with and through me, even when I'm afraid. Amen.

45

Becoming Fearless

Even when I walk through the darkest valley, I will not be afraid, for you are close beside me. Your rod and your staff protect and comfort me.

PSALM 23:4 NLT

I ONCE READ A DEFINITION OF FEAR THAT called it *the belief that something bad is going to happen.* And I said to myself, "Yeah, that's true." Then I realized that *faith* is the belief that something *good* is going to happen (Hebrews 11:1). Faith and fear both involve belief, and they both involve believing things we cannot see. A guy once told me that he didn't believe in God, because he couldn't see Him. So I asked, "Do you believe in fear?" That question changed everything for him.

I never want fear to be a problem for me again. If even the tiniest fearful thought sneaks in, I want to be able to say no to it immediately. That's why I had the word *Fearless* tattooed on the inside of my left arm, where I can see it best. And in the earlier days, when the anxiety attacks would still hit, I would physically grab it and hold on. That tattoo is my permanent reminder that God has defeated fear so that I can live fearless.

Getting a tattoo itself can be a scary experience. You know, needles on the skin and all. But amazingly, I wasn't the slightest bit afraid. (That would have been pretty ironic to freak out over a "Fearless" tattoo.) In fact, I was so happy that I could hardly keep from laughing. If I look closely, I can see a place where the tattoo artist actually messed up because I was shaking with laughter.

But you should know that my tattoo isn't a trophy to commemorate a permanent victory over fear. It's actually only the beginning of the war. Because fear will challenge us again and again. It's good to celebrate each time we break free from fear, but it's also important to remember that things aren't going to stop being scary. My tattoo is just a message to me and to everyone who sees it that I'm not going to stop living fearless because I am taking God at His word.

Becoming fearless is both an achievement and an ongoing journey. For me, it's also a commitment and a way of life. I pray it will be the same for you.

Lord, there are many things that scare me, but I trust You more than the fear. I pray that I would be aware of Your presence in the face of fear so that I, too, can live fearless. Amen.

46

On a Dark and Stormy Night

Praise the LORD, my soul. LORD my God, you are very great; you are clothed with splendor and majesty. The LORD wraps himself in light as with a garment; he stretches out the heavens like a tent and lays the beams of his upper chambers on their waters. He makes the clouds his chariot and rides on the wings of the wind.

PSALM 104:1–3

I USED TO BE TERRIFIED OF TORNADOES and other natural disasters. Don't get me wrong; there are times when it's natural to be afraid of those things, especially if you've ever experienced one yourself. But my fear would kick in with every flash of lightning or puff of wind. It was not rational, and I struggled with it for years.

One night I stayed with a friend who lives near Nashville, Tennessee. It was January, and the wind was ferocious that night.

This was no ordinary winter wind; it was so strong I could hear it inside the house, and it really scared me.

At that time in my life, I was serious about my journey out of fear. I had learned not to freak out over the weather or other things that sparked my anxiety, but to pray or read God's Word. So I picked up my Bible, asked God to speak to me, and could hardly believe what I read. Yep, Psalm 104:1–3. When I read that God "rides on the wings of the wind," everything changed for me. Now I love the wind because it reminds me of God.

God took something that had caused me to be afraid for years, and in just a few minutes, He showed me that I didn't have to fear the wind at all. In fact, I could find strength and comfort in it. God always finds a way to speak into your stuff.

He'd been speaking into my stuff for a long time through His Word, but I didn't know it, because I didn't open the Book! The power of God's Word and the comfort of the Holy Spirit were there for me all the time; I just had to look for them.

When you see something God created, remember His qualities—His power, His creativity, His love. And when you think on these things, you can overcome your fears and gather the courage to step into God's purpose for your life.

———————

Lord, Your Word tells me that all creation
sings Your praises. Teach me to hear
that song and to sing along. Amen.

47

Keep Moving Forward

Now there is no condemnation for those who belong to Christ Jesus. And because you belong to him, the power of the life-giving Spirit has freed you from the power of sin that leads to death.

ROMANS 8:1-2 NLT

WHEN WE BREAK FREE FROM FEAR, THE Enemy will often try to make us feel ashamed or upset about the ways we once allowed fear to control us. I've been through that, and so have lots of other people. We let fear keep us from doing something fun. We even let fear keep us from doing something for God—and, at the time, it seems perfectly reasonable.

Author and activist Christine Caine once said something that I find really relatable: "So often, we are paralyzed by the fear of missing God's will. We literally do not move because we are waiting for 10 confirmations. Here's the deal, most times you are going to have to step out in faith, to find out if it's God. God is big enough to redirect you if you're wrong."[1]

Once we get out from under fear's control, though, we

realize we didn't escape something frightening; we missed out on opportunities to have fun and to serve God. We realize how crazy fear is, and we find ourselves filled with regret over our fear-based decisions. We can even allow those regrets to hold us back from doing other things. If we're not careful, we might stop being a slave to fear and end up being a slave to shame and regret instead.

These are real struggles, but we have to remember that walking with God will set us free not only from fear but also from regret, shame, and anger. When we embrace the new life Jesus offers us, we can say, "Okay, Lord. I'm sorry I let fear run my life for so long. I'm sorry I missed out on some great opportunities that came my way. But I believe shame, regret, guilt, anger, and every other negative emotion and lie of the Enemy were dealt with at the cross. You died to set me free—not just from sin and death but also from these feelings of condemnation."

Don't look back. Keep moving forward into the freedom Jesus died to give you. Don't let fear hold you back from the amazing life He has planned for you.

Holy Father, through the sacrifice of Jesus, You offer me a new life. I receive that life now, Lord, and all the freedom that comes with it. Lead me and guide me. Amen.

48

Slap Fear in the Face

I can do all things through Christ who strengthens me.

PHILIPPIANS 4:13 NKJV

ON JUNE 7, 2018, I JUMPED OUT OF AN airplane that was going 140 miles per hour at 14,000 feet above the ground.

Let me explain.

In the days leading up to this, I decided that fear had been writing the story of my life for too long. So I started doing some things that once made me afraid—on purpose. Every time I did, boldness rose up in me. So I asked myself, "What could I do to slap fear in the face?" Immediately I thought of skydiving.

Now, don't think I'm encouraging you to skydive or to go do something completely crazy. What I'm talking about is facing a fear. Your fear may be as simple as introducing yourself to someone, deciding to pay your way through college so you can get a degree, or stepping out and living your faith boldly. Maybe you have a fear of never losing weight, so you join a gym, or you have a fear of always being in debt like others in your family, so you hire a financial advisor. Whatever your fear, find a way to face it.

As I thought about skydiving, my emotions screamed, "No way!" But I knew that making that jump was only going to increase my confidence. So I decided to go for it. My mom and my friends even decided to jump with me.

As the plane took off, the guys at the skydiving place started making jokes about what could happen if our parachutes didn't open. They were simply joking with us, but I later realized that they were doing exactly what fear does. Fear taunts and tries to intimidate us. But when our hearts are established in the freedom God has given us, we can laugh at the fear of the future.

Don't let fear have the final say in your life. Don't even give it a vote. Don't let it steal your adventure with Jesus. As actor Will Smith once said, "God placed the best things in life on the other side of fear."[1] What can you do to slap fear in the face?

Lord, I don't want fear to steal the adventures You have planned for me. Show me how I need to overcome fear—and then give me the courage to do it. Amen.

49

So Do Not Fear!

"So do not fear, for I am with you; do not be dismayed, for I am your God. I will strengthen you and help you; I will uphold you with my righteous right hand."

ISAIAH 41:10

IF ANYONE KNEW HOW TO PUT THE POWER of God's Word to work in her life, it was my great-grandmother. Even when she was very old and could not remember much, she remembered and drew strength from Isaiah 41:10.

My great-grandmother had a strong Southern accent and a dramatic way of speaking. She believed this verse with all her heart, so when she said it aloud, she said it slowly, with conviction and passion. It's almost like she put an exclamation point after "So do not fear!" Then she stretched out the word *I* for two or three beats. Every time she said it, she was emphasizing that *God* is the One who is with us, that *He* is our God, that *He* strengthens us and helps us, and that *He* upholds us with His righteous right hand. We can't do any of these things for ourselves. God does them for us, and we can trust Him to do them.

I can quote this verse word for word because my great-grandmother said it to us for years. And the funny thing is, now it's hard for me to say this verse without imitating her sweet voice. As her health declined and she knew her life was coming to an end, she said it more than ever. I think it was her way of finding comfort in her last days. She was speaking God's Word over herself, using it to find strength for her journey to heaven.

But what I'm not sure she knew is that every time she said it, she was giving *us* comfort and strength as well. She was bringing the power of God's Word to work in our lives, and that's the best gift she could have ever given us.

We will all go through hard times in life. We may lose jobs, possessions, and people who are dear to us. We can even lose our way and our sense of purpose in God's kingdom. It's in those moments that we need a hope beyond this world to cling to. We need a promise we can know will never fail. And, thankfully, through the Word of God, we have exactly that. So we do not fear.

Holy Lord, Your Word offers so many promises.
Help me not only to claim each one in my life
but also to pour them out on others. Amen.

50

The Stuff of Legends

Be strong in the Lord and in his mighty power.

EPHESIANS 6:10

HERE'S A SITUATION YOU MAY RELATE TO . . . no shame. Imagine you're back in fifth grade gym class, and the P.E. teacher says it's time to pick teams for dodgeball. Now, you're good at plenty of other things in life, but just imagining this scenario is giving you anxiety. You're smart, and you have a great personality, but throwing and dodging balls is not your thing. You know you'll be the last person chosen, and you just pray you get on the right team—the team with the most athletic guy in your class, the one who always leads everyone else to victory. But you don't. Instead, you get picked for the worst team in the history of the world. The one with a full roster of non-athletes like, well, *you*. Maybe that sounds dramatic, but in that moment, it really feels that way.

Now that you have that situation in mind and you're remembering the feelings that go with it, let me say that it reminds me of the dramatic tale of David and Goliath—a battle between a

Philistine hero with bodybuilder muscles and a sharp sword, and a pip-squeak of a boy with nothing but a slingshot. Their fight became the story of a champion versus a legend. It probably goes without saying, but Goliath was the champion and David became the legend.

You may think a champion and a legend would be fairly similar. But with one, people talk about you for a day, a week, or maybe a few months. With the other, people are still telling stories about you long after you're gone.

So, yeah, maybe you weren't the person everyone picked to be on their team. Maybe people still don't see much potential in you. But just because you don't look like a champion, that doesn't mean God can't help you become a legend.

There is something legendary inside of you. God put it there Himself. The process of becoming a legend will mean facing some fears, but the more you walk with God and let the Holy Spirit lead your life, the more your legendary-ness comes out.

Will you commit to becoming a legend in your world? I know, it sounds daunting and you may be thinking, *That's so not me!* But trust me—you've got the stuff of legends inside you.

———————————

Lord, I'm so thankful that I don't have to look like a champion to the world so that I can leave a legacy for Your kingdom. Help me to fight for Your glory—not my own—in every battle I face. Amen.

51

It's About God

Whatever you do, do it all for the glory of God.

1 CORINTHIANS 10:31

THERE'S SOMETHING ABOUT THE STORY OF David and Goliath that's easy to miss, but it's something I just love: when David stepped out to fight Goliath, he gave God the credit for his win before the battle even started.

Notice what David said to Goliath:

You come to me with sword, spear, and javelin, but I come to you in the name of the LORD of Heaven's Armies—the God of the armies of Israel, whom you have defied. Today the LORD will conquer you, and I will kill you and cut off your head. And then I will give the dead bodies of your men to birds and wild animals, and the whole world will know that there is a God in Israel! And everyone assembled here will know that the LORD rescues his people, but not with sword and spear. This is the LORD's battle, and he will give you to us! (1 Samuel 17:45–47 NLT)

Before David loaded the stone into his slingshot, he was already telling everyone around him that God would get the credit when he defeated Goliath. He basically said to Goliath, "This is about God. You has spoken against God, and that's not okay. I'm fighting in the name of God, and God Himself will conquer you. I'm going to slay you with this slingshot and cut off your head. But this isn't about me. It's about God, and this is His battle to win."

Fighting godly battles should give you confidence because anytime you're on God's team, you can know that you already hold the victory. But God's people don't take credit for those victories. They know their successes rest on the fact that God has created them and given them their skills. They understand that no matter how wonderful their accomplishments may seem, they couldn't pull them off alone—God is in every victory. And they happily give Him credit and thanks.

As you step into the purpose God has for your life—as you follow Him into victory over your fears—remember who you are, who God is, and what He has done for you. Then give Him all the glory.

Lord, any good there is in me and any good I have done is only because You are with me. Guide me this day, God, to bring glory to Your name in all I say and do. Amen.

52

Sometimes You've Gotta Fall

I was pushed back and about to fall, but the Lord helped me.
The Lord is my strength and my defense; he has become my
salvation.

PSALM 118:13–14

SOMETIMES YOU'VE GOTTA FALL. LITERALLY.
Because that's how you learn to get back up and keep going.

I read somewhere that if you fall in public, you will get up
twice as fast. Once, my best friend busted it on the corner of a
very busy street. Someone actually rolled down their window
and screamed, "Safe!" as if she'd slid into home base on the
concrete. But as painful as the fall was, because people were
watching, she bounced back up as if it were nothing.

Getting back up faster in public is not only true for a physical
fall but for an emotional one too. It's kind of like learning to walk.
To us as adults, walking is like breathing. We don't even think
about it. But unlike breathing, we actually had to *learn* how to

walk. Recently, when my two little nephews were learning to walk, my mom talked about how important it was to *let* them fall. Why? Because if they never fell, they'd never learn how to get back up again.

Now maybe you're thinking, *That's cute and all. But what do babies learning to walk have to do with me and God?*

Here's the thing: you're still learning to walk with God. We all are. That means God will sometimes allow painful things into our lives that knock us flat. Because He wants us to learn how to get back up and keep walking with Him. That's what happened with Job. He was the richest person in the land of Uz. But God allowed the devil to take away everything Job had, including his children, livestock, and wealth. Job was knocked down but kept trusting God. And after a time, God blessed Job even more than before. (Read the book of Job for the full story.)

The key is to keep walking *with* God. To keep praying, studying, trusting, and obeying. We can't handle the tough times—the cancers, the divorces, the lost friends, the betrayals—on our own. They knock us flat. But when we trust God to help us, we can get back up and keep walking. And this time, we'll be walking even closer to Him.

———————————

Holy Father, when tough times come into my life, when I fall, teach me to stand back up and walk even closer to You. Amen.

53

Sing Your Song!

Sing to the Lord a new song, for he has done marvelous things.

PSALM 98:1

WHAT GIVES YOU LIFE?

What stirs up your passion and energy?

What do you love so much that you forget to eat when you're doing it?

That's what makes your heart sing. And if you want to really live, part of the answer is to find your heart's song and sing it out with everything you have.

As for me, I like to sing, but I'm insecure when it comes to singing in front of an audience. So when it was time to record the opening worship song for the first Live Original tour, I surprised even myself when I said I'd sing it. The next thing I knew, I was standing in a studio wearing headphones with a microphone in my face. But here's the thing: I knew *nothing* about recording studios.

An hour into the recording, the producer asked me if I was hearing the clicks okay. (Soft clicks play through the headphones to keep you on beat.) My response was, "Oh, yes. They are driving me crazy! I've been trying to tune them out"—which completely explained my continued off-timing belt-outs. I didn't know what the purpose of the clicks was, so I was just winging it, and it was *not* working.

Eight hours later the recording was done. I asked the producer how many times it takes "normal" recording artists to get their songs, and he said it typically takes around eight to twenty times.

"Okay, cool. So how many times did it take me?"

"Two hundred eleven."

My whole team busted out laughing, including me. Even though I felt like I had just taken 211 face-plants in front of everyone, we all believed that this song was so much bigger than that. It would be an anthem for people to declare that they are a part of the family of God.

What's my point? It's okay to laugh at yourself as you do the things God has called you to do. Take some risks. Face-plant. But don't bury the talents and gifts God has given you because of the fear of failure. What song have you been waiting to sing? Find a way to sing it—today!

———————

Holy God, please give me the courage to
sing the song You created me to sing—
and to sing it with all my might! Amen.

54

If You're Carrying the Football . . .

A heart at peace gives life to the body, but envy rots the bones.

PROVERBS 14:30

WHEN WE START LIVING WITH MORE CONFIDENCE and boldness, when we start speaking words of life and truth, our lives begin to look different. And that's when jealousy can rear its ugly head. My family describes it like this:

"If you're carrying the football, you're going to get tackled."

Let me add that jealousy is not just a girl problem or a twenty-first-century problem. Just look at the book of Acts, when the church was first getting started. Notice that every time a crowd formed, so did jealousy.

In Acts 5:12–16, the apostles were healing crowds of people—that's something to celebrate! But Acts 5:17–18 says that "the high priest and all his associates . . . were filled with jealousy." Followers of Christ were arrested, abused, and forced to leave because of what? Jealousy! Instead of celebrating all that the apostles were doing, the crowds met them with jealousy. But let's be honest: Don't we sometimes do that to people too?

The jealousy from others can be enough to make us want to drop the football so we won't get tackled, but that's not the life God invites us to live. Standing against jealousy is hard, but it's possible. God has given you gifts, and He wants—*expects*—you to use them. If He blessed you with a beautiful voice, then sing, even if some criticize every note. If you're good at organization and leadership, then lead a project, even if others second-guess your decisions. And if you were created to teach, then get out there and tell everyone you can about God's amazing love. Yes, even if they tackle you like you're carrying the football for the winning touchdown of the Super Bowl, at least you're playing in the Super Bowl! Pastor and author Rick Warren once said, "Criticism is the cost of influence. As long as you don't influence anybody, nobody's going to say a peep about you. But the greater your influence . . . the more critics you're going to have."[1]

If you have ever felt the sting of jealousy, follow Paul and Barnabas's example from Acts 13:51–52: shake the dirt off your feet and walk on with joy, knowing the Holy Spirit is with you.

———————————

Lord, when I feel the sting of jealousy,
help me to do as the apostles did—and
keep on joyfully serving You. Amen.

55

Do *Not* Give Up

I cling to you; your strong right hand holds me securely.

PSALM 63:8 NLT

A FEW YEARS AGO I HIT A LOW POINT, A *really* low point. I was coming out of a brief but tough relationship that ended up hurting my heart pretty badly. I also had a ton of things going on with work and travel. A lot was happening at once. I had been hiding the depth of the pain I was feeling from everyone close to me. That only made it harder to bear because I felt that the only place I could be fully human and cry was in the car. I knew that when I reached my next destination, I would just laugh it off quickly and say, "All is well."

I tend to think I am a pro at pulling myself together, but this time I really didn't know how I could do that. That's when I had the most terrible thought—a thought I struggle to even type out. But I want to be real with you about the places our minds can take us when we are hiding and running to the point of deep exhaustion.

I actually thought, *If I had a wreck right now, I don't think I would mind. I need a hard break no matter how I get it.*

I didn't really mean that. I didn't want to end my life, but in that moment, a month in the hospital in a body cast with other people taking care of me didn't seem so bad.

But right after my mind "went there," within a split second I caught a glimpse of the moon. It was huge that night, and I sensed the Lord saying, *Sadie, this world is a lot bigger than you. If you want to quit because you think your problems are too great to handle, then you will lead many others to do the same.*

On any given day, you may be super stressed and really want to take a break from everything. But please know that you're worth a lot more than your feelings will tell you. One day—no matter how rough it is—does not define your life. Your purpose and calling give you an important place in the world. Do *not* give up. Hold tight to God. There is so much more joy to come and so many people counting on you to keep going.

Lord, sometimes I feel like I've been beaten up by this world. Comfort and shield me, and hold tight to me as I try to hold tight to You. Amen.

56

Epic Fails

The LORD directs the steps of the godly. He delights in every detail of their lives. Though they stumble, they will never fall, for the LORD holds them by the hand.

PSALM 37:23–24 NLT

THERE'S ONE THING YOU CAN BE SURE OF: you will not do everything right. At some point, you'll have an epic fail, or you'll at least make a mistake or do something others think is funny or stupid or weird. People will notice, and some of them won't let you forget it.

If you do anything that involves other people in any capacity, you "risk" being roasted. I put quotation marks around "risk" because it's not just a possibility. It's more of a fact. There will be times all of us will be picked on or made fun of. I say that not to be a downer but to say this: don't let the fear of being roasted stop you from doing something you are excited about doing!

People roast people. Think about the person that you are a huge fan of. Odds are if you go to their social media account, no matter how great they are, there will be some roasts in the comments. It happens to me all the time. There are YouTube videos out there with hundreds of thousands of views where I'm being verbally picked apart. There are hundreds of comments saying that I sound annoying when I talk. Do those things hurt me? Sure. Because I'm human, and sometimes the comments sting. But I don't let those little stings stop me from doing what I love to do and from using my voice in the spaces where God opens doors for me to speak.

Don't let the fear of being roasted stop you either. Don't be silenced because a group of people are choosing to focus on your mistakes or point out qualities that aren't your best when you could be saying something that could change someone's life and affect eternity. You don't want the haters to hold you back from fulfilling your purpose.

If you have a desire in your heart to do something, but you're afraid you'll be roasted, I say do it anyway! If negative comments come, then they come. But don't let that stop you from doing what makes you, *you*! And certainly don't let it quiet your voice!

Lord, knowing that everybody fails doesn't make it any easier. So I pray that You would give me the courage to keep doing what You want me to do—even if it means getting roasted. I pray Your voice would be louder than the hate. Amen.

57

It's Just Being Happy

Celebrate God all day, every day. I mean, *revel* in him!

PHILIPPIANS 4:4 MSG

YEARS AGO, SOME FRIENDS AND I DECIDED to choose a word to focus on for the next twelve months, and I chose *celebration*. Everyone else was choosing words like *surrender, sacrifice, build, faith*—you know, really serious words. Some of my friends laughed because they didn't think my word was very spiritual. Plus, I celebrate all the time. I love to throw a party for no reason. So it didn't really seem like a word that would bring much challenge to my life.

But one definition of *celebrate* is to "honor or praise publicly," and I've been thinking about this a lot as I read the Bible.[1] The book of Revelation paints the most amazing picture of God's throne. Surrounding Him are twenty-four elders, and in the center are four living creatures who *never* stop worshipping Him (Revelation 4:8).

My takeaway from this is that because I know my God is holy, I can publicly honor and praise Him—no matter what my day looks like. I can celebrate when everything is going well, but I can also celebrate when things are not so great. There were nights that I struggled to celebrate because of how I was feeling. So I would literally go outside, look at the stars, and worship Him because He is always worthy of my praise.

There were times within that year that I would think, *Shoot, why did I pick this word?* Here is a small example: I took a trip that had me traveling from Israel to Ohio to Colorado, but my bag never showed up. *Never.* Not in Israel, Ohio, or Colorado. I had to be on camera and speak in front of people, and I had *nothing.* I spent two weeks borrowing everything from literal strangers, and I mean *everything.* When I finally got my bag back, my suitcase was destroyed, and my hair products had burst and stained my new clothes. Let's just say I was challenged by what my response was going to be. I ended up bleaching my clothes and laughing about it. To this day, I get complimented on those bleached clothes.

It's easy to let the bad stuff steal your celebration. But if you look at the big picture, you can find a way to celebrate. It's not being naïve; it's just choosing joy and celebration as a strength. What can you celebrate today?

Lord, I pray that You would help me to see all the reasons I have to celebrate today—and don't let me forget to thank You for every one. Amen.

58

Connecting the Dots

The LORD himself goes before you and will be with you; he will never leave you nor forsake you. Do not be afraid; do not be discouraged.

DEUTERONOMY 31:8

I NEVER WAS VERY GOOD AT CONNECT-THE-dot pictures. I didn't have the patience for them, and I thought some of the dots were unnecessary. Give young Sadie a coloring book and crayons any day, but *please*, not a connect-the-dot drawing.

Now that I'm older, I still don't always like to connect the dots, but I've learned that it's necessary if I want to be free, strong, and happy. If I want to live with a sense of adventure and purpose, I can't draw my way around any of the dots life throws at me.

If you're wondering, *What on earth is she trying to say?* I can explain. Not long ago, it dawned on me that what God does in our lives is like those connect-the-dot pictures. You see, God has a specific purpose for each of us, and He maps out our journeys so everything in our lives moves us closer to that purpose. Though we can't see where life will take us, He can. And He knows every little dot we need to go through in order to shape us into who we're meant to be. There's the character-building dot, the realize-you're-unconditionally-loved dot, the learn-to-find-peace-in-life's-storms dot, the make-Jesus-the-king-of-your-heart—no-really dot, and all kinds of others.

Some dots seem enormous and black, and you don't know if you'll ever find your way out of them. Some dots are smaller and easier to see your way through. As you get older, you'll look back and eventually realize that with God, there are no unnecessary dots.

What's your dot right now? No matter how it feels, I challenge you to commit to going all the way through it. Embrace it, deal with it, pray about it, and find scriptures that will help you handle it in a godly way. Why? Because on the other side of your dot is something so amazing and so beautiful that it would break your heart to miss it.

God, help me connect the dots and go through each one with the confidence that You are walking with me, fighting for me, healing me, and making me stronger and freer every step of the way. Amen.

59

Exhaling Your Ugly

He has rescued us from the kingdom of darkness and
transferred us into the Kingdom of his dear Son.

COLOSSIANS 1:13 NLT

UGLINESS—FEELINGS OF FEAR, JEALOUSY,
disappointment, and unworthiness—has a way of getting trapped
inside of us, and we need to get rid of it. From my own experiences, I've learned seven steps that help me deal with my ugly,
and I call it "exhaling my ugly." This isn't some kind of formula
that automatically works. But if you use it as a general guide and
follow the Holy Spirit as He guides you, He will ultimately lead
you to the breakthrough that will change your life. So here are
the steps:

1. **PRAY LIKE CRAZY.** When God sees that you want His
   help, He'll give you all the help you need.
2. **TELL YOURSELF THE TRUTH.** You can't tell the truth
   to God or others until you first tell it to yourself. Admit
   how you feel.

3. GET YOUR PAIN OUT. Write, draw, dance, sing, go on a good drive, or find some other way of releasing what's bottled up inside of you.
4. ASK GOD TO HEAL YOU. Once you surrender your situation to Him and ask Him to heal you, you'll begin to see Him working in your life.
5. SHARE YOUR HEART WITH SOMEONE YOU TRUST. Having a friend pray with you and for you is a game changer.
6. OPEN YOUR HEART TO HEALING. God's healing isn't always easy. Embrace it by praying something like this: *God, I choose to open my heart to whatever You need to do to make me whole and strong.*
7. BELIEVE GOD'S WORD. His Word is the most effective weapon on earth to defeat the lies the world tries to get you to believe. Let it strengthen you and tell you how beautiful and valuable you are to God.

If ugliness is hiding inside you today, take a deep breath . . . and *exhale.*

Holy Father, I take a deep breath here and now, in Your Presence, and I release to You all the ugliness inside me. Heal me, Lord, and seal me with Your Spirit. Amen.

60

Just Four Words

Draw near to God and He will draw near to you.

JAMES 4:8 NKJV

SOMETIMES WHEN WE'RE TRYING TO LIVE our lives fully, we go wrong by turning to quick, temporary highs. We try to satisfy ourselves with things that will leave us high and dry instead of simply filling our lives with the promises of God, which are guaranteed. We try to fill the empty spaces in our hearts, the gaps in our lives.

The expression "fill the gaps" means "to add what is needed to something to make it complete"[1] or "to serve temporarily."[2] To say that a gap needs filling is to say that something is missing, but I'm telling you, if you've given your life to God, you already have all you need to fill your heart and soul; you just have to realize it.

What does "fill the gaps" mean for you? Diet pills to make yourself feel beautiful? Sleeping around to make yourself feel loved? Sending inappropriate photos or editing your pictures to make yourself feel desirable? Pornography to make yourself feel satisfied? Addiction to make yourself feel numb?

If you are involved in these things, have you found that you can't stop because the rush is the only thing that keeps you going? Have you discovered that these activities never fill the gaps and always end in pain, fear, emptiness, and feelings of worthlessness? Ephesians 5:11 says, "Do not participate in the worthless and unproductive deeds of darkness, but instead expose them" (AMP). If you have been participating in worthless things, I want to tell you this: you are not worthless, but those things are worth so much less than who you are.

You are already loved, already enough, already seen, and already known *just as you are*.

Because God is love, and God is enough. He created you, formed you, and is with you just because you are His. This is your reality—God is the only One who can fill the gaps.

It's time to get back the fullness of your life. Maybe you're thinking, *Sadie, I'm throwing my life away. How do I get to God from here?* I'll offer you one tidbit of advice. It's just four words, so don't miss it:

Turn in His direction.

———————————

Lord, please show me who I really am—and how You fill in all the gaps in my life. Amen.

61

Believe *for* Yourself

"'Father, I was wrong. I have sinned against you. I could never deserve to be called your son. Just let me be—'
The father interrupted and said, 'Son, you're home now!'"

LUKE 15:21 TPT

I ONCE LED A BIBLE STUDY FOR GIRLS IN A juvenile detention center. I asked them, "What changes do you hope to see in yourself when we finish our study?"

The first girl said, "I don't want to be so mean anymore." Everyone laughed because she was mean all the time. "Yeah, right," they said. "Who are you if you aren't mean?"

I stopped them, saying, "Whoa. Whoa. Everyone chill. All of you, tell her you believe it will happen for her." Still laughing, and not really believing, they said, "I believe that for you."

The next girl said, "I don't want to go back to drugs." She spoke with such authenticity and vulnerability that the whole room shifted. The other girls then knew exactly how to respond as they said somberly, "I believe that for you."

Sometimes what stops us from getting back on the right

path is what we believe about ourselves. This is especially true when our mistakes have led us into places we never thought we'd be, and shame makes it hard for us to believe good things are in our future.

Think about the prodigal son in Luke 15. He demanded that his father give him his inheritance. Then he ran off and wasted it on drinking and partying. When the money was gone, so were all his new so-called friends. He ended up with a job feeding pigs and was so hungry he wished he could share their food. What do you think he thought about himself at that point? I'm guessing it wasn't good. He had hit rock bottom so hard that he was ready to crawl back home and beg to be his father's servant—not his son. He couldn't get past what he believed *about* himself—that he was an epic failure unworthy of his father's love. So he couldn't even begin to believe something *for* himself—that he'd be welcomed back home as his father's son.

If you let the bad things you believe *about* yourself—and that others believe *about* you—define your life, that's a tragedy that will paralyze you. It will keep you from moving forward. Start making a list of the good things you can believe *for* yourself, and know that just as that father welcomed his son home with open arms, God will welcome you.

Holy Father, show me any lies in what
I'm believing for myself and teach me
the truth about myself. Amen.

62

Come Home

The faithful love of the LORD never ends! His mercies never cease.

LAMENTATIONS 3:22 NLT

I'D LIKE TO REIMAGINE THE PARABLE OF THE lost son, found in Luke 15:11–32 (and I've taken a lot of creative liberties!).

A father gave each of his two daughters a share of his wealth. The oldest saved her money, stayed close to her family, and worked in the family business. But the youngest saw her inheritance as her "ticket to Hollywood." The day she turned eighteen, she set out to live the life she wanted. She thought, *I'm young and rich. These are the best years of my life. I should do everything I want to do.* So she filled her life with alcohol, drugs, and partying.

When she ran out of money, her so-called friends disappeared. Desperate, she found herself doing things she never thought she'd do. She even contemplated suicide because she was so exhausted, lonely, and filled with shame. Then she thought about all the people who worked for her father. "Even they are better off than I am!" she cried.

I'm not worthy to be my father's daughter, she thought. *But I have to go home to survive. At this point, I'd be glad just to scrub the floor of what used to be my home.*

As she made her way back, she stopped at the coffee shop in her hometown where she had often gone when she felt lost. She was almost to her regular spot when she looked up and saw her dad. Before she knew it, she was wrapped in her father's arms, and he was on his phone planning a welcome-home party.

"No, Dad. Stop," she said. "You don't know what I've done. I'm no longer worthy of this kind of love."

But he said, "You are my daughter. Nothing you do could change that. You are safe, forgiven, and altogether beautiful. This will always be your home!"

If you're feeling lost, go back home—you may think God is mad at you, done with you, or upset with you, but the reality is He's just waiting for you to come home.

Lord, when I'm lost and feeling alone, forgive me of my sin. Help me get past my shame and remember that You are always waiting to welcome me home again. Amen.

63

Wandering

I'll never forget what you've taught me, Lord, but when I wander off and lose my way, come after me, for I am your beloved!

PSALM 119:176 TPT

HAVE YOU EVER NOTICED THAT THE BIBLE has a lot of stories about wanderers and wanderings? And these wanderings usually weren't good experiences. Think about it. In the Old Testament, the Israelites spent *forty years* wandering around in the wilderness to make what should have been an eleven-day journey. While it might be easy to judge them, how many times have we spent years dealing with the same problem that could have taken days to solve if we had listened to God? In the New Testament, the prodigal son wandered all over the place, walking on the wild side wherever he went, before he finally returned to his father's house (Luke 15).

I think we all have a little bit of a wanderer in us. Don't we all get off the path of life at times? Don't we all let our hearts and minds stray from God and from His Word on occasion? Sure we do—and when it happens, what matters most isn't that we've wandered but that we *get back on track with God.*

Ideally, we would be so in love with God that when we wander, we would end up back in His presence right away. We would hunger so much for Him that our wanderings would take us closer to Him, not farther. But it doesn't always work that way. Sometimes we keep on running from God until He sends someone or something to stop us and help us find our way back to Him.

I want to encourage you today, if you have wandered away from God, to get back to Him. Pull out your Bible and start reading it again. Today is the day. Begin to talk to God in prayer again and be looking for His answers. Reconnect with your Christian friends. Find someone older who loves and walks with God who is willing to mentor you and help you grow stronger in your faith. Go back to church, where you can learn about God and worship Him.

Don't wander one second longer. God is waiting to welcome you home.

Holy Father, forgive me for the times I've wandered away from You. I choose today to be devoted to You, sold out in my faith, and committed to knowing and living by Your Word. Amen.

64

When the Middle Schooler Leaves You in the Dust

I press on to reach the end of the race and receive the heavenly prize for which God, through Christ Jesus, is calling us.

PHILIPPIANS 3:14 NLT

IN HIGH SCHOOL I WAS GOOD AT THROWING the javelin and shot put, so the track-and-field coach asked me to join the team. "Okay," I told him. "But I can't run."

"You can just do field events," he said. So we had a deal.

But as our team prepared for our regional meet, the coach said, "I need some of you to compete in events you don't normally do." We needed the points to make sure we would go on to state. He then said, "Sadie, you'll do the two-mile."

Everyone started laughing, including me (at first), because I thought he was joking. I was the only person in that whole circle of people who didn't even run the warm-up laps—not even once. I should have been the last pick!

"Why is that funny?" the coach asked.

When an authority figure wants to know why something is funny, what you thought was hilarious just moments before is no longer funny.

As soon as that race started, I knew it would not end well. Everyone lapped me, including a middle schooler. Ouch. Which led me to the horribly embarrassing realization that I was going to have to run the last lap all alone, with everyone watching.

As I started the final lap, I heard the first lines of my basketball warm-up song playing out of nowhere. I turned and saw my brother John Luke heading straight for me with the song playing on his phone. He had come down from the bleachers to run that last lap with me! The crowd went wild! I loved it! My brother completely took away my humiliation.

What John Luke did for me that day was a perfect picture of what Jesus does for us all the time. He meets us in our embarrassments and failures, and He redeems our story.

If you're feeling humiliated for some reason right now, I want to encourage you. Don't stop when it gets hard. Don't let the most painful part of the story become the end of it. Keep moving ahead, even if you go slowly. Trust Jesus to redeem your story!

Lord, there are days when I feel like I've been lapped by a middle schooler. But I will trust You to use even those days to make my faith stronger. Amen.

65

Messed Up, Now What?

If we confess our sins, he will forgive our sins, because we can trust God to do what is right. He will cleanse us from all the wrongs we have done.

1 JOHN 1:9 NCV

JESUS SAID IT WOULD HAPPEN. PETER SAID it wouldn't, but it did. After Jesus was arrested, Peter denied knowing Him three times—just as Jesus said he would do. And after that third denial, "immediately a rooster crowed" (John 18:27 NKJV). The Bible tells us that Peter "went out and wept bitterly" (Luke 22:62 NKJV). Peter had messed up. And he knew it. So what did he do? He went back to his old life. He went fishing.

That's what a lot of us do, isn't it? When we mess up, we go back to where we were before Jesus. And sometimes it's a lot worse than fishing. We go back to the partying, the drinking, the relationship, the sex, the lifestyle that we had before the Savior came into our lives.

And we think, *Maybe this time it will fill me up.* Remember what happened to Peter, though? When he went back to fishing, he kept throwing those nets out and pulling them back in, and they were empty every time (John 21:3). He got nothing. When we go back to those old ways of living, we get nothing—nothing that fills us up. Those old ways don't really satisfy, even though they might have once tricked you into thinking they did. After you've experienced the fullness of Jesus, the world feels very empty.

Notice that Peter didn't do anything to get back to Jesus. Peter was out on the boat fishing, and Jesus went to Peter. It was Jesus who said, "Hey, let's have breakfast." And they had breakfast at a charcoal fire—the same kind of fire where a cold and confused Peter denied Him (Luke 22:55). Jesus is a redeemer. When we mess up and go back to our old, sinful ways, Jesus comes after us. First John 1:9 says, "If we confess our sins, he will forgive our sins, because we can trust God to do what is right. He will cleanse us from all the wrongs we have done" (NCV).

Not only will Jesus forgive you, but He will also give you a place and a purpose in His kingdom. It's what He did for Peter, and it's what He'll do for you.

Holy Lord, forgive me for the times my words and my actions have denied You. Forgive me, and use me to tell the world about You. Amen.

66

Someone Who'll Tell You the Truth

The heartfelt counsel of a friend is as sweet as perfume and incense.

PROVERBS 27:9 NLT

FRIENDS ARE WONDERFUL. THEY LISTEN TO us, validate our feelings, and often tell us exactly what we want to hear. But sometimes we need more than that. We need a mentor—someone who's willing to tell us when we've gotten off track, who'll tell us the truth. Godly mentors provide three things friends don't always offer: (1) they won't judge, (2) they won't validate feelings that don't align with God's Word, and (3) they will cover the lies you've believed with God's truth.

There was a time when I was struggling desperately, and I suddenly felt an overwhelming conviction to share with my mentor the pain that had been hiding inside of me. I needed to tell her some of the things I had been struggling with that were holding my heart captive.

As I talked to her, she did the most amazing thing: she simply began to speak truth from the Word of God. Every verse or biblical principle she shared with me brought light into my heart where darkness had lived for so long. As she shared the Word and prayed for me and with me, I began to see the lies for what they were—complete untruths. And as the Word of God brought light to my mind, those lies began to unravel and no longer held me captive. I began to see a new side of God and develop a deeper relationship with Him.

I pray that God will bless you with a godly mentor in your life. Someone who will help you see what is truth and what is not. But let me say this: the key to a breakthrough is not looking to a mentor; it's looking to God. That's where healing is. A good mentor will point you to His Word, not just their own.

If you are wondering if you can ever find freedom from your pain, I encourage you to start by looking to God and repenting of your sins. Seek out someone you trust, like I did, and make a turn toward God. It's a necessary step toward living out your purpose. I don't know what your journey will be, but I believe with all my heart that God has freedom for you and that you'll find it.

Lord, I pray that You will bring someone into my life who will help me keep looking to You. And I pray that You would help me to be that person for someone else. Amen.

67

Step Up and Declare

He said to them, "But who do you say that I am?"
Simon Peter answered and said, "You are the Christ, the
Son of the living God."

MATTHEW 16:15–16 NKJV

ONE OF THE LOVE LANGUAGES IS CALLED
words of affirmation. To *affirm* something means to state that it
is true. That is my number-one love language.

Sometimes in your relationship with Jesus, you need to
affirm some things. Why? Because the Enemy is going to want
to steal your truths from you. He wants to make you wonder and
doubt and question. Think about Peter when he was with Jesus
at that breakfast on the beach. Three times Jesus asked Peter if
he loved Him (John 21:15–17). And three times Peter said, "Yes,
Lord, you know that I love you" (v. 16).

Now, Jesus knows everything that is in our hearts, so He
knew that Peter loved Him. Why all the questions then? Because
Peter needed to say it out loud. Peter needed to hear himself say

the words. Peter needed to *affirm* the truth of his relationship with Jesus. And so do we.

Today, I want you to affirm your relationship with Jesus so that you don't question it anymore. So that you don't search for what only He can give you—or what He's already given you, like His love.

Think about your past for a moment, about those things you wish you'd never done that still hang over your head. Confess them and let Him redeem them, forgive them, and wash them away. His grace is so huge and so good, there's no shame. Accept His love and forgiveness.

And now let's affirm some things. I'm going to ask you the questions that Jesus asked Peter, and each time I want you to answer out loud. Hear your words of affirmation.

"Do you love Me?" *Yes, Lord, I love You.*

"Do you love Me?" *Yes, Lord, I love You.*

"Do you love Me?" *Yes, Lord, I love You.*

Whether you're just getting to know Jesus or you've been a Christian your whole life, affirm this truth that you love Him. Do it as many times as you need. And whenever the Enemy challenges your path, step up and declare, *I know that I love Jesus, and I know that He loves me.*

Holy Father, fill me with the truth and power
of Your love for me and my love for You. Amen.

68

It's a Private Call

Very early in the morning, while it was still dark, Jesus got up, left the house and went off to a solitary place, where he prayed.

MARK 1:35

BECAUSE I SPEND SO MUCH TIME IN THE public eye, people seem to think that my life with the Lord is mostly lived out in public. That's not true, nor do I ever want it to be true. My relationship with God really is lived out in private. What you see in public is the overflow of who I am in private. It is the same for you.

I asked my dad what advice he would give to anyone thinking about seeking any kind of fame. He said, "Whoever you are now, you will just be a magnified version of yourself in public." Simple, yet something I don't think everyone considers.

If you're greedy, selfish, jealous, or angry in your private life, you will be a magnified version of that on TV. Because you can't hide who you are. In the same way, if privately you're reading, studying, journaling, and soaking in His Word, then the Lord is going to be magnified. Because "the mouth speaks what the heart is full of" (Luke 6:45). When you spend time in private hearing and meditating on the whispers of God and His Spirit, then that's what's going to flow out of your lips in public.

When Christian and I started dating, we decided not to announce our relationship to the public for the first six months. In the past, I had announced other relationships right away, and then they didn't work out. I think part of the reason they didn't work out—besides the fact that they weren't the right ones for me—is that we were not yet confident in our private relationship before we let the public speak into it. I'm so thankful Christian and I developed a secure relationship and confident trust in one another before the whole world knew. It's helped us stay authentically and purely in love in the midst of the busy and public days. It is the same for your relationship with God.

Whether you want to live your life in the spotlight or simply live for God right where you are, I encourage you to study, pray, and respond to the Lord in your personal space in order to develop a steady relationship. Your time with Him in private will bless you and enable you to be a blessing to others.

Holy Father, remind me that this life You've called me to isn't about putting on a show for others to see; it's about living for You even when no one is watching. Amen.

69

What It Means to Truly Live

Surely your goodness and unfailing love will pursue me all the days of my life, and I will live in the house of the Lord forever.

PSALM 23:6 NLT

I LOVE WORDS, AND I LIKE TO UNDERSTAND them better through their definitions. So let's take a minute and talk about the word *live*. In addition to "remain alive," to *live* is to "make one's home in a particular place or with a particular person."[1] A synonym for this is *reside*. Let's keep it simple by combining those two and saying that to *live* is "to remain and to reside." But what does that look like in real life, remaining and residing?

First, to *remain* means to "continue to exist, especially after other similar people or things have ceased to do so."[2] Maybe you have been trying to remain in things that will not last instead of things that are eternal. Maybe the job you thought would last forever let you go, you had to move, your parents got divorced, your friends left, you broke up, or the season changed. The thing you put your security in crumbled, and now you don't know what your life is. It can be tough to remain when it seems like everything else is falling apart around you. So how do we remain alive? By remaining in the One who never changes.

The other part of our definition of *live* is "to reside." Because of Jesus' sacrifice, you have a place where you belong. You get to reside in God's house forever. Ephesians 2:19 (MSG) paints a powerful picture of this:

> You're no longer wandering exiles. This kingdom of faith is now your home country. You're no longer strangers or outsiders. You *belong* here, with as much right to the name Christian as anyone.

Jesus invites you into His Father's house, a safe place to reside. I encourage you to say yes to that invitation. Say yes to life and find out how it can be so much more than remaining alive. Because it's time for you to truly *live* in His presence and in His purpose for you.

Holy Father, help me to truly live by finding my identity in You and not in the cheap copies and temporary fixes of this world. Amen.

70

Already Approved

We have been approved by God to be entrusted with the gospel [that tells the good news of salvation through faith in Christ].

1 THESSALONIANS 2:4 AMP

WHEN CHRISTIAN AND I FIRST STARTED "talking," there was no pressure. Because there *is* no pressure in DMing or texting or talking on the phone. But when we started dating and the words "I like you" came out, I started to get a little nervous. All of a sudden, I was pulling out my A game. I was getting my nails done, and, y'all, I went so far as to get a spray tan each time before he visited. I mean, I was *extra*. This is really embarrassing to admit, but I even started practicing the dance moves I was going to do in the car on the way to our date. Why? Because I wanted him to like me.

The word *like* means to be enjoyable, to be found agreeable, to bring satisfaction. In social media terms, it's about winning someone's approval. So you can see how striving to be liked could create a lot of pressure. In those early days of dating

Christian, I felt like I needed to win his approval, so I was doing my best to make sure he liked me.

Sometimes we think we need to do the same thing with God. We try to bring our A game in order to get Him to like us, in order to win His approval. We strive to be perfect. Then when we mess up (because you know we all do!), we go through the whole "I don't know if God really likes me because I did *this* or *this* or *this*." Or "He might be mad at me because I don't read enough, pray enough, serve enough."

Hear me when I tell you that God is not like that. You don't have to win His approval. You don't have to try to impress Him. He's not sitting up in heaven saying, "Hold up, Jesus. No mercy and forgiveness, no love for her until she gets it right." No! God already sent His Son to save you because of how much love He has. He knows you're not perfect. He knew all about you before the foundation of the world (Ephesians 1:4). He knit you together in your mother's womb (Psalm 139:13). And get this: His approval isn't granted by what *you've* done but by what Jesus has already done for us! And He wants you to share that great news with others.

Holy Father, thank You for loving
me just as I am. Amen.

71

Don't Waste the Waiting

Those who wait on the LORD shall renew their strength; they
shall mount up with wings like eagles, they shall run and not
be weary, they shall walk and not faint.

ISAIAH 40:31 NKJV

ONE DAY I WAS SITTING IN A COFFEE SHOP,
talking with my best friend and enjoying a coconut latte, my
favorite in the whole world.

A guy came up to our table and said he wanted to ask me
something. But he didn't want me to give him the same answer
his pastors and friends had given him. No pressure, right?

"I am super frustrated with God," he said. "I grew up in a
Christian family, and I did my best to walk with God. But my
brothers and sisters didn't even try to follow the rules. They were
accepted at the colleges they wanted, and now they have the
jobs they want. But I didn't get into the college I wanted, and I
don't have the job I want. Every time I ask someone why things
have turned out this way for me, they say, 'You are just in a season
of waiting.'"

He wanted me to give him a different answer, but I couldn't. And the truth was that this guy wasn't simply frustrated with waiting; he was angry that everyone else seemed to be getting what he believed he deserved.

Doing "everything right" doesn't mean we'll get everything we think we deserve, and it doesn't stop us from having to wait. The waiting season doesn't have to be wasted time, though. I think many of us view it as a waste because we tend to be unproductive when we wait. I mean, is it just me or does everyone knock out some levels of Candy Crush while waiting at the doctor's office? Okay, maybe that's just me, but you get the point that waiting can feel useless. But it's different with God. If you're waiting on a relationship, use that time to draw closer to God, to be the whole person He made *you* to be. If you're waiting on the perfect job, focus on being the best worker you can be right where you are. If you are waiting on a friend group, be the friend to others that you want to find. There is purpose in the waiting.

There's so much we could be doing and so much God *is* doing in our lives, even in seasons of waiting. Don't let frustration cause you to miss that. Ask God to show you how you could be growing in this season of waiting.

Lord, I understand that sometimes You have things to teach me while I wait. Help me to listen and learn while I wait. Amen.

72

Is God's Plan *Really* Going to Be Better?

"Blessed are those who trust in the LORD and have made the LORD their hope and confidence."

JEREMIAH 17:7 NLT

I'M NOT GOING TO LIE TO YOU. WHEN YOU walk in the world's ways, yes, it can look cool and exciting. And, yes, sometimes it is fun. But that doesn't mean it will fill your soul.

You might remember that my family had a TV show. It was successful, and because of it, I was able to do some things I wouldn't have gotten to do otherwise. But I have to tell you that without a purpose or finding your identity in God, those things can be really empty. Sure, *Dancing with the Stars* was fun, but not knowing who I was while so many judged me gave me anxiety and insecurity, even in the middle of one of the coolest times ever. Don't get me wrong—I loved the experience. But the anxiety and the lack of control I felt I had over my life at the time led me down a bad path.

I finally realized, *Yeah, these cool experiences are great, but there's got to be something more.* I reached out to Jesus to find my identity and His plans for me. I remember asking the Lord why He was putting me in those positions. I was searching for a way to make it all make sense. I was searching for my purpose. Shortly after, I began preaching about Him. It started in the simplest way. I made a YouTube video—preaching to myself, really. The next thing I knew, it had millions of views. That's when I realized that the platform and the pain had a purpose.

Do I still have hard days? Absolutely. No matter what you do, you will face challenges. But when you are doing what the Lord calls you to do, then you get to do it all with Him. You will find love, joy, and peace in the midst of challenges as you walk out your purpose with God.

So if you're looking at what the world has to offer and what God has to offer, and you're wondering if God's plan for you is going to be better, let me tell you, the answer is *yes*! A thousand times yes!

Don't let the world distract you. Don't let the critics and the haters stop you. God has plans for you.

—————————

Lord, I believe You have a plan for my life, and I believe it is the best for me. Help me have the courage to trust and follow You. Amen.

73

Get to Know God

He says, "Be still, and know that I am God."

PSALM 46:10

DURING THE CHRISTMAS SEASON, NO SEVEN-year-old says, "You know, I can hardly wait for Christmas because I'll get to spend quality time with my family and sing Christmas carols with the people I love."

No. The mind of a seven-year-old thinks, *I told Santa I want an Easy-Bake Oven, and if it's not under the tree, then I don't believe in him anymore.*

We can treat God the same way when we are not mature in our relationship with Him. We can easily think, *I told God I wanted that, and if He doesn't give it to me, then I am not going to believe in Him anymore—or at least I won't trust Him.* A healthy relationship with God doesn't work that way. The relationship comes first, and God's response—whether it's the one we want or not—gives us an opportunity to grow in our relationship with Him.

I need to tell you this, and maybe it's going to be hard to hear, but God doesn't promise to always give us what we want.

He does promise to give us strength when we're weary (Isaiah 40:29), to never leave us alone (Deuteronomy 31:8), and to give us a rich and full life (John 10:10).

When you've asked God for something and then find yourself waiting for Him to respond, don't let the seemingly slow response pull you away from Him. Realize that the timing of His answer is perfect, even if you can't see that right away. See that time as a gift that will allow you to invest in your relationship with Him. Get to know His character and who He is. Search His Word, pray, and seek His presence just to be with Him, not for what He might give you. That's how it's supposed to work, but sometimes we flip it around. Today, praise God for who He is. And declare to Him—and yourself—that all He has already done is enough for you.

Lord, so many times I come to You with a list for You to bless me with this, help me with that, and protect me from this. But today I simply want to be with You and learn who You are. Amen.

74

The Dance of Your Life

Those who are led by the Spirit of God are the children of God.

ROMANS 8:14

WHEN I WAS ON *DANCING WITH THE STARS*, I learned that to be confident in your dancing, you have to be confident in your partner, trusting that he will lead you where he is going. When I watched the show when I was growing up, I always thought it was so much easier for the guys because the girls could cover them by dancing around them. Being there, though, I realized it actually might be easier for the girls to learn how to make a beautiful dance together, as long as they have a good partner, because the male is the leader.

Many times Mark, my partner, would give my hand a little push or pull to make sure I was back to the original dance and on track for the next move. He could do this because the dance was his masterpiece, his creation. He knew it better than anyone, and more than anyone, he wanted it to be the best it could be. So I learned how to follow that push or pull. I trusted that he knew how to lead me because he created the dance.

It's the same with your life. God created you. He wrote your story. He also extends His words and His love to lead you, and He will not lead you where He is not going. When you dance down your path of life with Him, He may tug you or pull you in a direction, and it's *vital* to fully embrace that next move confidently, knowing He is pushing you into the step He made just for you.

Because God created you, He knows exactly how to lead you in the dance of your life. All you have to do is pay attention to the nudges and follow Him. Trust that He knows how to make the dance of your life more beautiful than even you do.

———————————

Lord, I surrender myself completely to Your leading. I trust You to guide me through the dance You have planned for me. Amen.

75

Skip the Likes

God demonstrates his own love for us in this: While we were still sinners, Christ died for us.

ROMANS 5:8

HERE'S A FUNNY STORY. MY RELATIONSHIP with my husband, Christian, started with a follow. You see, a few years ago, we were both at a Passion Conference. He saw me and messaged me on Instagram. It was a really sweet and kind message. It was also pretty bold. He was not shy about the fact that he was definitely interested in me. But here's the thing: I didn't see that message until two years later.

One night Christian and I met in person, and I thought, *I'll give him a follow.* I looked up his Instagram, and the second that I followed him, I got this little message notification. I thought, *Wow! That's fast.* Turns out I was really slow. So I crafted my own message. I thought I'd just say something funny like, "Sorry for the late reply. Lol," but I sent a nice message back because secretly I was interested too. That was the start of our relationship.

You know how the process goes after that. First, it's DMing, then texting, then talking on the phone. Finally, we go on a date, but we're not official. Then one day, we're official. And that's when those three little words start coming out. Not the big words. It's the "I like you" words.

Of course, no one wants to stay in the "I like you" phase. In fact, most of us tend to rush through that phase, but not Christian. "I like you" became "I *really* like you." Then "I like you *soooooo* much." After about two months of all these different ways of saying "I like you," I was like, "Would you say it already?" But there's a process (longer for some than others!) to get to the "I love you" stage. And it's a much-needed process when we're evaluating who we're going to be with.

But the amazing thing is, there's no process with Jesus. He skips it all and jumps straight to the "I love you" phase. Jesus doesn't need to get to know you better or check out His options. He's already head-over-heels, come-to-earth-and-die-on-a-cross-to-save-you, crazy in love with you.

So quit worrying about your options in the world. Skip the whole "I like you" phase with Jesus, and commit to a relationship with Him, knowing you are loved.

Holy Lord Jesus, thank You for loving me, even with all my mistakes, with all my imperfections and problems. Thank You. Amen.

76

Warmed by God's Word

Open my eyes to see the wonderful truths in your instructions.

PSALM 119:18 NLT

FOR THREE YEARS PETER FOLLOWED JESUS. Not the social media kind of follow from afar. Peter literally walked right beside Him. They were close. Best friends.

Then one night, when Jesus' ministry on earth was about to come to an end, He tried to explain to Peter and the other disciples what was coming. He told them He was going to a place where they could not follow, at least then (John 13:33). Peter did *not* like this. "I will lay down my life for you," Peter said. But Jesus answered, "Very truly I tell you, before the rooster crows, you will disown me three times!" (vv. 37–38).

Later that night, when the band of soldiers and priests came to arrest Jesus, Peter rushed out and cut off a guy's ear. He proved he was ready to lay down his life for Jesus. But when Jesus stopped him and let Himself be arrested, confusion set in. Peter and all the other disciples ran away.

Let's give Peter some credit, though. He came back. He went

all the way to the high priest's courtyard (John 18:15). That's when the Bible says something interesting: "It was cold" (John 18:18). So Peter stood near the fire, warming himself.

When our faith is cold and we're confused about our relationship with Jesus, that's usually when the toughest challenges come. Peter didn't understand God's plan for Jesus at the moment. He was confused, and their relationship felt a little cold. So when the servant girl said, "Hey, weren't you with that guy, Jesus?" Peter let the cold and confusion do the talking and said no—three times.

So many times, we encounter God at Christian events and get a spiritual high. But when that runs out, we get cold in our faith and start to wonder where God is. Peter was just in an extreme version of that.

Feeling far away from Jesus can lead to making decisions we later regret—even to deny Jesus. But just because your faith feels cold or you're confused, do not assume that He is not with you. He is. Trust Him. Trust His plan. Don't warm yourself at the world's fires because they don't last. Warm yourself and your faith with His Word. It will spark a fire that never stops burning.

———————

Lord, when I don't understand, help me
to trust and follow You anyway. Fan
the flame of my faith daily. Amen.

77

Running and Hiding
from God

Where can I go from your Spirit? Where can I flee from your
presence?

PSALM 139:7

IT WAS JANUARY 16, 2017, THE BEGINNING OF
the Winter Jam tour. I sat in a hotel room at a beautiful beach
resort, and instead of enjoying the views or hanging out with
people, I sat on my bed and wept.

I welcomed the tears because for nearly a year prior to that
day—since I went through a hard breakup—I had not been able
to cry. I had held a lot of pain and regret in my heart and hidden
it from everyone around me, even God. I knew that God sees and
knows everything, but I didn't want to address the hurt swirling
in my heart. I was running from Him as hard as I could, trying
to hide the ugliness inside me. I shut down my feelings, sucked
everything up, and put on my game face, which did not allow
for tears. I was so ashamed that I never told anyone about those

hurtful things that were circling around my mind and heart. I thought that if I buried them so deeply that I couldn't see them, they wouldn't hurt me anymore, right? No! I found out that day that the hurts we try to cover up in our hearts get infected and inflamed, and they affect us in more negative ways than we realize.

That night the Holy Spirit showed me that I needed to admit my hurts honestly to God, hold nothing back, and allow myself to feel the pain they caused. Then I needed to release it all to Him, ask Him to heal it, and receive His healing work.

So I got out a notebook and started writing. I poured everything out that was hurting me. With each word, I prayed for freedom. I hate to tell you this, but it didn't happen with a bolt of lightning from heaven or the voice of God pronouncing my release from the pain. But it did begin that day when I stopped hiding my true emotions from God. David set the best example in the psalms he wrote, showing us that it's good to be real with God. That's the beauty of a close relationship with unfailing love. You get to be fully *you*, right where you are.

Are you running from God? Hiding something inside you, even from Him? Grab a notebook and start writing. Because when you let God in, that's when His healing begins.

Lord, forgive me for the times I run and hide from You when what I most need is to run right to You. Please heal me of the hurts inside. Amen.

78

Not Too Crazy to Pray For

Help me overcome my unbelief!

MARK 9:24

SOMEONE ONCE TOLD ME SOMETHING THAT changed my life and the way I pray: "Sadie, you just need to ask God to give you the faith to believe."

I heard those words at a time when I was toeing the line between saying yes to what God had called me to and staying comfortable. Those simple words struck me, convicted me, and made me think, *Ask God for faith?* Before I heard that encouragement, I had felt that the one thing I could do for God was to have faith. I knew that He could give me peace and joy and other things. In fact, He has given me everything. He has sent His Son for me. Couldn't I at least give Him faith? I thought my job, so to speak, as a Christian was to have a lot of faith and a lot of hope and to believe and not doubt.

But then I realized that in the New Testament, even the apostles said to Jesus, "Show us how to increase our faith" (Luke 17:5 NLT). And then there is the story of the father in Mark 9.

His son had been possessed by a demon for *so* long, and the disciples had not been able to cast it out. So when the father came to beg for Jesus' help, he doubted Jesus could do it either. When Jesus said, "Everything is possible for one who believes," the father begged, "I do believe; help me overcome my unbelief" (Mark 9:23–24). Jesus didn't scold either the apostles or the father. He taught them, and He helped them.

The Lord *wants* to help us strengthen our faith. He understands it's hard to believe sometimes. So if you're struggling with faith, I encourage you to ask God to give you the faith to believe. You can also pray that He will give you the strength that you need or that He'll help you believe that you are loved and that you are enough. Or maybe it goes deeper, and you need to ask Him for the faith to believe that your life matters and your breath has purpose. That's not too far-out to ask God for. That's not too crazy to pray for. It's exactly what God wants you to do.

What do you need to ask God for in your life and faith?

───────────

Holy Father, You ask me to believe and to have faith—and that is what I want to do—but I need You to help me do that. Help me to have faith. Amen.

79

The Question You Never Have to Ask

Nothing can ever separate us from God's love. Neither death nor life, neither angels nor demons, neither our fears for today nor our worries about tomorrow—not even the powers of hell can separate us from God's love.

ROMANS 8:38 NLT

I'VE BEEN TO JUVIES, PRISONS, CHURCHES, colleges, middle schools, and high schools, and I get this everywhere I go: "Sadie, because of what I've done, I need to ask this: Do you think Jesus still loves me? Do you think I should even try to have a relationship with Him? Is there still a purpose for me? Is Jesus still an option for me after what I've done?

They're the questions we never have to ask because the answers never change. Yet we always seem to end up asking, *Jesus, do you love me?*

We ask the question because we know what we've done. We know we haven't lived up to His standard. If someone treated us the way we have treated Jesus, chances are, we wouldn't love them. That's because our love as humans is often contingent on what someone does for us. But with Jesus, we have to remember His love is based on what *He* has already done for us. So we find ourselves asking, *Jesus, do you love me?*

So let me answer that question right now. Yes! A thousand times, yes! Jesus loves you. He knows exactly what you've done— probably even better than you know yourself. And He loves you anyway. And He has a purpose for your life anyway.

God's love is not confusing. It doesn't change based on what you do or don't do. You never have to worry about losing His love. However, that doesn't mean you can just go out and do wild things because God loves you. Yes, He is loving, but He is also just. I know Christian loves me and always will, but I am not going to go sin outside of our marriage and just say, "Well, you should love me anyway." Because of how much I love Christian, I would never want to hurt his heart. It should be the same with God.

You've probably heard the verses from 1 Corinthians 13: "[Love] bears all things, believes all things, hopes all things, endures all things. Love never fails" (vv. 7–8 NKJV). Those words describe God's love for you. Think about that. Let that sink in. *His love for you never fails.*

Holy Father, Your love is so huge that I don't understand it, but I claim it, I rest in it, and I praise You for it. Amen.

80

Choose Life!

"I am the way and the truth and the life. No one comes to the Father except through me."

JOHN 14:6

I LOVE TO KNOW ALL MY OPTIONS. EVEN with something as simple as a meal, I want to know what my choices are. I want to think through all the restaurants that are available. When I get there, I even ask the waiter what he or she thinks the best option is for my meal.

There's one decision I've already made, though, and I don't need to think about my options anymore. That's the choice between life and death. Because those are our two bottom-line options, and what we decide determines everything about how we live.

Most of the time, when people talk about life and death, they're speaking in physical terms. If someone has a heartbeat, her brain is working, and she can breathe on her own, we say she is alive. When those organs fail, a person is dead—technically.

But when I use the words *life* and *death*, I'm talking about the spiritual, emotional, relational force inside you and whether that leads to happiness, hope, light, strength, confidence, purpose, passion, success, peace, and fulfillment (life) or whether it leads to misery, despair, darkness, weakness, insecurity, worthlessness, apathy, failure, and feeling restless and unfulfilled (death).

I'm a girl who likes options, and I've found the only one that leads to life: Jesus. He is "the way and the truth and the life" (John 14:6). You can choose life through Him.

Look at what God says about it: "Today I have given you the choice between life and death, between blessings and curses. Now I call on heaven and earth to witness the choice you make. Oh, that you would choose life!" (Deuteronomy 30:19 NLT). Part of what I like about this verse is that God is saying, "These are your options—life or death, blessings or curses." Then He tells us exactly what He wants us to do. It's almost like He is begging us—*begging you*—to make the right decision when He says, "Oh, that you would choose life!"

So let me ask you this: Are you choosing life?

Lord, thank You for giving me the option to choose life with You. Help me to choose it over and over again with each decision I face. Amen.

81

Turn Up the Contrast

For the creation waits in eager expectation for the children of God to be revealed.

ROMANS 8:19

ONE NIGHT I WAS AT A CONFERENCE, AND the speaker said something that really hit my core. She said that as believers, we are called to be people of contrast. I think she meant that when we are living as people of the light, our lives will look different from the lives of people who live according to the world's values.

When I think of contrast, I think of the edit function when picking out a photo filter. We spend a lot of time editing photos to get the contrast to the right percentage, even though no one would ever notice the difference in our pictures unless we turned the contrast all the way up. This made me think about how I would spend so much time worrying about things I couldn't change, filling my mind with things that aren't positive, watching shows that aren't beneficial to me, and listening to music that didn't leave me inspired.

So I started weeding those things out of my life. Instead, I spent more time investing in things that made me grow, learning from people who are way ahead of me on life's journey, listening to things that inspire me, and reading things that change my perspective in a positive way.

I challenge you to keep a log of the ways you spend your time this week and ask yourself for each item, *Is this helping me live the life I want to live? Is this helping me grow?* Then think of the ways you want to grow—the direction you want to go. What good contrast do you want to make in the world? Do you want to be generous in a world that withholds? Kind in a world that makes fun? Deep in a world that's shallow? All about relationships in a world that's all about advancement? Start looking for ways to spend your precious time on activities that educate, expand, and encourage you—things that give you life instead of death. Make little choices today to turn up the contrast.

Holy Father, show me today how I can turn up the contrast in my life so that all the world knows I belong to You. Amen.

82

Watch What You're Spilling

"I have the right to do anything," you say—but not everything is beneficial. "I have the right to do anything"—but not everything is constructive.

1 CORINTHIANS 10:23

MODERN-DAY TEA PARTIES AREN'T THE KIND our grandmothers went to—where ladies dressed up and drank hot tea and ate sandwiches with no crusts and talked about polite things. No, we have lost the class in our "tea parties." You all know what I am talking about, don't you? When someone walks in the room and says, "I'll spill the tea."

"Spilling the tea" is typically code for "I've got some gossip I cannot wait to share." I was wondering one day why it's so hard for us to not spill the tea. Why is gossip such a struggle? And I started thinking about why it is a struggle in my own life. If I am being really honest with myself and all of you, 99 percent of the time when I'm feeling the need to gossip, it's because I am feeling insecure. Why do we think it will make us feel better about ourselves to talk badly about someone else?

People like to be "in the know," and they like to be the first to share really good information. The problem is that "really good information" isn't always really good for everyone to know, especially if you don't even know if it's true. If it's not true, it could really hurt someone and do all kinds of damage you never intended. Even if it is true, it may not be something other people need to know.

The wise and mature thing to do when you just can't wait to share all of someone else's stuff is to ask yourself, *If this situation were happening in my life, would I want the whole world to know about it?* If you wouldn't, then don't share it. Resist the urge to spill the tea.

Spilling the tea (aka gossiping) doesn't seem like a big deal when you are doing it to other people, but if you have ever been in the middle of it, it feels like a pretty huge deal. It hurts, and it's never worth the pain it will cause.

Let's bring some class back to our tea parties. Choose your words carefully because they have the power of life and death. Do you need to change the way you speak to and about other people?

Lord, when I am tempted to gossip about others because of my own insecurity, I pray that You would help me to choose kind and helpful words instead. Amen.

83

Eighty-Five-Year-Old Friends

Gray hair is a crown of glory; it is gained by living a godly life.

PROVERBS 16:31 NLT

IT'S REALLY NICE TO HAVE AN EIGHTY-FIVE-year-old friend. Mine is my great-grandmother, Mamaw Jo.

Mamaw Jo was born in the 1930s—when Franklin Roosevelt was president of the United States, before World War II broke out, and before Jeeps were invented. She's seen a lot—and learned a lot—during her lifetime. But some things rise to the top when all the trappings of life fall to the ground. Things like . . .

- LIVE IN THE MOMENT. Relax and enjoy the good times God gives you instead of using them to craft the next social media post.
- SURROUND YOURSELF WITH LAUGHTER AND THE PEOPLE YOU LOVE, AND YOUR DAY WILL BE A GOOD ONE. Mamaw Jo laughs every chance she gets. She's built

her life on faith and family, and when people do that, they can find something good in every day.

- LET PEOPLE KNOW HOW HAPPY YOU ARE TO SEE THEM. The fact that Mamaw Jo is always glad to see me makes me feel so special and loved. I try to remember that I can make other people feel special, and you can too!
- SEE PEOPLE FOR WHO THEY ARE BECAUSE WE ARE ALL JUST HUMANS. Mamaw Jo understands that no one is better than anybody else. She knows nobody is perfect except Jesus. She doesn't let anyone's attitude determine how she treats him or her; she's going to be kind no matter what.
- SURROUND YOURSELF WITH CHEERLEADERS, FOR THEY WILL CHEER YOU ON TO BE THE BEST VERSION OF YOURSELF. Mamaw Jo is a huge supporter of whatever I do. As much as she does that for me, I also want to do that for others—to listen, care, support, and encourage them.

Who's your Mamaw Jo? Find a way to thank that person. And if you don't have that person in your life, then be that person for someone else.

Lord, thank You for the people—of all ages—that You place in my life. Help me to soak up their wisdom and learn from their love. Amen.

84

Real Friendships Don't Just Happen

Ruth replied, "Don't ask me to leave you and turn back. Wherever you go, I will go; wherever you live, I will live. Your people will be my people, and your God will be my God."

RUTH 1:16 NLT

WE ALL NEED FRIENDS. THEY HELP US LIVE out our purpose. Lots of Bible verses talk about the value of friends, like "two are better than one" because "one can help the other up" (Ecclesiastes 4:9–10) and "a sweet friendship refreshes the soul" (Proverbs 27:9 MSG). But friendships don't happen without any effort on our part. Real friendships happen because we make them happen.

Look at Ruth and Naomi. Yeah, they were mother-in-law and daughter-in-law, but they were also friends—the kind who stick together in hard times and support and encourage each other. Let me give you a quick summary of the story.

A famine caused Naomi, along with her husband and two

sons, to move from Bethlehem to the land of Moab. Her sons married two Moabite women, Ruth and Orpah. Long story short, the husband and sons died, and Naomi decided to head back home to Bethlehem. She urged Ruth and Orpah to go back to their own families. Orpah did, but not Ruth. She left everything behind—her family, her home, the world that she knew—to go with Naomi to a land that hated Moabites. Her vow of friendship holds some of the most beautiful words in the Bible. "Wherever you go, I will go; wherever you live, I will live" (Ruth 1:16 NLT). Ruth refused to leave Naomi's side when things got hard. And she was later blessed for it with a home and child of her own. Her friendship with Naomi led her to her purpose.

It's easy to be a friend when it doesn't require anything of us other than having fun. But real friendship is about sticking together in the good times and the bad, the times when one of you moves away, when one is celebrating and the other is mourning, and when one succeeds and the other fails. Real friendship is listening, helping, and encouraging, even when it's not easy or convenient. It takes time, and it takes work. But a real friendship is one of the greatest treasures on earth. Be intentional and create that kind of friendship.

Holy Father, I pray that You would bless me with a real friend and that You would teach me to be that kind of friend. Amen.

85

Quit Camping Out

We take captive every thought to make it obedient to Christ.

2 CORINTHIANS 10:5

MY TWO-MAMA (MY MOM'S MOM) HAS ALL kinds of wise little quotes and sayings. One of them is "Quit camping out in your mind."

"Camping out in your mind" simply means focusing on a certain thought, usually a negative one, and staying there—like you pitch tents in a campsite. That indicates you aren't leaving anytime soon. You intend to stay a while and soak up the experience. Camping out around the wrong thoughts never turns out well, and it can lead to real trouble.

When a scary, negative, lustful, envious, or doubtful thought first works its way into your brain, you have a choice. You can camp out on that thought in your mind, or you can deal with it right away to keep it from becoming bigger.

I'll guarantee you, if you camp out on a negative or sinful thought long enough, the next thing you know you'll have another negative thought, then another, then another. And before you know it, you'll be drowning in fear, negativity, lust, envy, and doubt. Sometimes you just have to speak to your thoughts and tell them to line up with the Word of God. Here's an example: "I will no longer camp out on this thought that is bringing me anxiety. Jesus, help my mind to think on things that are true."

Probably the best Bible verse I've found to help with that is Philippians 4:8: "Fix your thoughts on what is true, and honorable, and right, and pure, and lovely, and admirable. Think about things that are excellent and worthy of praise" (NLT). My challenge to you right now is to memorize this verse. Post it somewhere you'll see it every day. I actually had it on my mirror for a while. Then, whenever you have a bad thought, remember these words and ask yourself, "Does this thought fall into one of those Philippians 4 categories?" If the answer is no, stop thinking it—quit camping out on it—and think about something that does.

God, help me to take captive every thought in my mind that is not of You and silence the whispers of the Enemy in my ears. Guard my mind with Your Spirit and truth. I choose to fill my mind with thoughts that are pleasing to You. Amen.

86

This Gives You Life

Your word is a lamp to guide my feet and a light for my path.

PSALM 119:105 NLT

IT'S TRENDY RIGHT NOW TO SAY, "OOOOOH, this gives me life!" about something—usually something funny—that gives you a little rush or makes you feel cool. I've said it at times too, but I think it's important to know what actually does give us life. Let's be real: when your life is on the line physically, you are not going to grab an Advil. It may make you feel better, but it's not going to give you life. A little pain relief does not equal real life!

I've experienced this firsthand. I used to try to make my pain go away or "fix" my life by going out with friends, getting a new outfit (or new boyfriend), or changing my hair. Unfortunately, I did some of these things in front of a large, public audience. I'm so glad God is a Redeemer! When I tried those things, I was happy for a moment and even had fun. But not until I truly connected with the source of life did I ever really *live life to the fullest*. When I say "connected with the source of life," I don't mean a scroll on social media. I mean a deep dive in the Word. I went from looking for life in places that could never deliver it in its fullness (because they were not designed to) to finding a consistent connection to joy by reading His Word.

The thing about a momentary rush is that temporary sources of life always run out. They quickly lose their appeal and aren't life-giving anymore. But some things *will* last for eternity, things we can always count on. These are the things of God, the fruit of who He is: love, joy, peace, patience, kindness, goodness, faithfulness, gentleness, and self-control (Galatians 5:22–23).

Take a deep dive into the Word today, and then you'll really be able to say and believe, "This gives me life!"

Holy Father, plant a longing in my heart for Your Word. And as I read it, I pray that You would help me understand its life-giving truths. Amen.

87

Just Sing

When times are good, be happy.

ECCLESIASTES 7:14

ONE DAY, TWO FIVE-YEAR-OLDS—CHILDREN of some friends of mine—were at my house along with their parents, and these two cuties asked me to play with them. We started to pretend we were worship leaders. Their parents are all worship leaders, so that's a pretty common game we play. And it is so cute! Not many things in life are cuter than kids worshipping.

Of course, the first thing anyone watching wants to do is take a video. But as soon as someone pulled out a phone, one of the kids said these words, which convicted me: "No, we are not supposed to take pictures. We are just supposed to sing."

We. Are. Just. Supposed. To. Sing.

My young friend knew more about life than the adults in the room did that day. There is so much freedom in living in the moment. Why do we have to stop the moments to snap a picture? Sometimes by doing that, we actually miss the essence of the moment, and we forget to sing. There are some friends that I have more pictures with than memories. These five-year-old children and I have hundreds of memories together and only one picture—which happened to be captured in a single moment when both of them ran into my arms for a big group hug. I love this picture because it wasn't planned, staged, stopped, or filtered. It was a priceless moment captured in action. These kids don't need a picture to capture the moment. They just live in it.

Now, I'm not hating on pictures. I *love* taking them. I take tons of pictures to help me remember the moments that are special to me. This is just a reminder to not let the picture-taking rob you of life's precious moments. Think about whether you're taking a picture for the purpose of showing it off or cherishing a memory. We need to stop thinking so much about the social media value of a photograph and start thinking more about the actual value of the experience.

Sometimes all we're really supposed to do is *just sing*.

Lord, remind me that sometimes I need to put down my phone and just enjoy the gift of the beautiful moments You place in my life. Amen.

88

One Really Big Fear

"Seek first his kingdom and his righteousness, and all these things will be given to you as well."

MATTHEW 6:33

I WAS THINKING ABOUT MY COLLEGE JOUR-ney recently and checked the internet to see what the biggest fears of college students are. I came across some information that shocked me: students are scared they're going to sacrifice their beliefs. They want to live according to their values, "but life has been very convenient for them, with little need to sacrifice for what is right," and they're not sure they can do it.[1]

Apparently we're afraid we're going to sell out an extraordinary relationship with God in order to fit in with the world. To be honest, this is crazy to me because we usually fear things that are out of our control. But in this case, we are literally scared of ourselves! Let's talk about this.

Many of us have had so few real challenges in life—the kind that blossom into a confident trust in the Lord and prepare us to stay true to Him even in the midst of our fears. And I'm talking about big fears here. Not just "I'm afraid I won't get along with my roommate" or "Should I take the new job?" or "Should I stay in this relationship?" And if we haven't faced big challenges before, stepping out into a new situation can be scary.

I think, ultimately, we need to change our posture as we walk into the world. Following God doesn't mean we say no to all of the "fun" things in life. Following Christ is the way to abundant life—to true joy and fulfillment. The things the world has to offer might be fun in that moment, but you'll end up with regrets and feeling empty inside. Walking out the purpose God has called you to—by loving Him, loving others, and obeying the Word—that's what will fill your soul. And I promise you, it is fun!

Living a vibrant life with God doesn't mean nothing will ever go wrong. Sometimes life gets really, really hard. But if you will choose to be the salt of the earth and the light of the world that Jesus calls you to be, if you will choose to celebrate all He has done in your life, you'll forget about trying to fit in with the world—and others may even want to fit in *with you*. When life gets hard, you'll be glad you have the rock of God to lean on instead of the temporary fixes of the world.

Holy Father, let my joy and my celebration
of You be so easy to see that others
will want to know You too. Amen.

89

What's That You Say?

When you speak healing words, you offer others fruit from the tree of life. But unhealthy, negative words do nothing but crush their hopes.

PROVERBS 15:4 TPT

I COME FROM A SPORTS FAMILY, SO I'VE heard a lot of cheers at football and basketball games. There's one cheer in particular that stands out to me. The first line is always different—usually something about how great the team is. But the next line is always the same: "What's that you say?"

"What's that you say?" is a great off-the-field question too. Being challenged about what we say is helpful because it makes us think about whether we are confident in the words we speak. Sometimes we say things we don't really mean. Stopping to think about what we're about to say can cause us to examine what's in our hearts and make sure our words align with it—and then make sure our words and our hearts align with our actions.

So I want to ask you today, "What's that you say?" I mean, what are you talking about—to yourself and to others? What kinds of actions are your words sparking? Are they bringing life or death? Are you confident in what you are saying?

Now I want to offer you a visual, so to speak, of what the words of life and the words of death look like:

The words of life <u>empower</u>. The words of death destroy.

The words of life <u>encourage</u>. The words of death cause people to lose heart.

The words of life <u>affirm</u>. The words of death tear down.

The words of life give <u>hope</u>. The words of death cause despair.

The words of life are <u>confident</u>. The words of death are powerless.

The words of life are <u>full of hope</u> for the future. The words of death replay the pain of the past.

Whatever purpose God has planned for your life, your words are critical to it. So examine what's in your heart and ask yourself, *Do my words bring life or death?*

———————

Holy Father, help me to pause before I speak and to examine my words. Let me always speak life and encouragement into every situation. Amen.

90

Bust Out Some Moves

Let them praise his name with dancing.

PSALM 149:3

MY FRIEND AND I WERE DANCING DOWN AN aisle in Walmart one day, and a seventy-six-year-old woman named Mrs. Elma—who we'd never met until that moment— came up laughing and said, "I just had so much fun watching you have fun in life. Not many people do that anymore. I have always told myself not to care what people think and to have fun, no matter what. If I want to dance in a store, I will dance. If I want to skip down a street, I will skip. Keep skipping through life, girls, and God bless."

I seriously believe that dancing is a universal language of freedom. On one of my trips to Haiti, I was walking with a group around the streets to support some local business owners who had just graduated from a program we were working with. As we were walking, a group of children began to follow us. We wanted to communicate with the children, but we didn't speak their language, and they didn't speak ours. Since I had nothing to say,

I just busted out some classic dance moves and then pointed at them. They laughed and repeated what I did. We ended up sharing dance moves back and forth for probably an hour and created great memories without ever saying a word.

Dancing is also a universal invitation. It enables people to become part of each other's lives because it brings people together. I remember on my very first date with Christian, we had a dance-off in a parking lot, and it was one of the first laughs we shared together. Dance is lively and expressive, and it can communicate all by itself. Dance offers a way to celebrate life, to connect with others, and, yes, to worship God in ways that words cannot. So the next time you're at a loss for words, consider busting out some moves.

Lord, give me the freedom and courage to dance so that I can celebrate life, connect with others, and worship You. Amen.

91

With Everything You've Got

"Love the Lord your God with all your heart and with all your soul and with all your mind and with all your strength."

MARK 12:30

I WANT TO LIVE MY LIFE WITH EVERYTHING I've got. In fact, I'd say that's how God *created* us to live. God's got big plans for each of us. And I don't know about you, but I don't want to miss out on one single moment of those plans. John 10:10 says that Jesus came to give us life. *Life!* Not just a *drag*-ourselves-out-of-bed-and-*drag*-through-the-day kind of life either. Jesus came to give us a life more amazing and filled with more purpose than anything we could ever imagine or dream of (Ephesians 3:20).

Is that the life you're living? And if it's not, are you ready to? Because living life with everything you've got doesn't start where you might think. And it definitely doesn't start where the world will tell you it does. Partying in ways that don't honor your body, doing whatever it takes to get all the "likes" on social media, sleeping around to make you feel loved? That's not the way to live the life Jesus came to give you.

So what is the way? You'll actually find it in a command. I know, I know, you're probably thinking, *The last thing I need right now is for someone to tell me something else I have to do*. But trust me, this isn't just someone; it's Jesus. And this isn't just any command. It's the greatest commandment: "Love the Lord your God with all your heart and with all your soul and with all your mind and with all your strength" (Mark 12:30).

In other words, the secret to living life with everything you've got is to *love God* with everything you've got. All in. Holding nothing back. Let Him have all of you.

Maybe you're thinking, *Sadie, there's no way I can love God perfectly like that. I have doubts. I have questions. I mess up too much.* Trust me, I get that feeling. But that's the amazing thing about God! You don't have to love Him perfectly. Just give God all the love, faith, and trust you've got—no matter how small it might seem—and He will meet you with His perfect love.

———————————

Holy God, help me to love You with everything I've got so that I can live for You with everything I've got. Amen.

92

Soak Up the Joy

You will show me the path of life; in Your presence is fullness of joy.

PSALM 16:11 NKJV

ONE OF THE BIBLE VERSES I LOVE IS PSALM 30:11, which says that God has turned our "mourning into joyful dancing" (NLT). This is something the Spirit of God does for us, and we can trust Him to do that within us. But we often think, *Okay, I know God turns mourning into dancing, but when is it going to happen?*

We can be tempted to believe that maybe God will turn our mourning into dancing after He responds to what we're asking for. I don't think that's necessarily true. I think God will turn our mourning into dancing when we simply rest in His presence, when we rest in the joy of who He is.

Joy is a fruit of the Holy Spirit (Galatians 5:22–23). It's something God provides for your life, and it can be with you every single day. That doesn't mean there won't be times when you are sad. Some situations are going to hurt; things are going to happen; friendships are going to change. Being joyful does not mean avoiding the circumstances that can bring pain or sadness. It means that during those hard times, there will be a deep inner joy that will continue through them. That is why joy is your strength (Nehemiah 8:10)! The Bible doesn't say that when everything in your life is amazing, you can have joy. It says, as the psalmist sings to God, "Your presence is fullness of joy" (Psalm 16:11 NKJV).

There is freedom, joy, peace, friendship, and relationship anywhere the presence of God is. You can worship, you can dance, you can be free, and, yes, you can rest—just because His presence is with you in the room.

Spend some time just hanging out with God today and soak up the joy.

Holy Father, I am so thankful that I can just sit with You and be with You anytime and anywhere. I pray that You will surround me with Your presence and fill me with Your joy. Amen.

93

Yeah, It Really Does Matter

Orpah kissed her mother-in-law good-bye. But Ruth clung tightly to Naomi.

RUTH 1:14 NLT

OUR CHOICES MATTER. AND SOMETIMES, they matter more than we realize in the moment.

Take the story of Orpah, for example. Remember Orpah? She and Ruth were Naomi's daughters-in-law. When they were all widowed and Naomi decided to go back to Bethlehem, Ruth went with Naomi. But Orpah chose a different path. She returned to her family's home in Moab. On the surface that doesn't seem like such a bad thing. She just went home, right? But the real choice was this: Orpah went back to the pagan gods of Moab, while Ruth continued on the path of following the one true God.

Ruth was blessed for her choices. She became the great-grandmother of David and even a great-great-I'm-not-sure-how-many-greats-grandmother of Jesus. But Orpah? Well, after she left Naomi, she disappeared from the Bible. I love a good story, though, and I was dying to know what happened to

Orpah. I found that Jewish tradition says she married and had four sons—all of whom were giants. And one of her descendants was named Goliath. Yep, some believe this is the same Goliath who was killed by David, his stone, and God.[1]

Now, we'll probably never know if that's what really happened to Orpah—at least not this side of heaven. But it does make an interesting point. Two women reached the same decision point in life, but they made two different choices with two very different results. One became the ancestor of a king and of the King, and one disappeared from the Word of God.

What does that mean for us? Our choices matter—and not just for a moment. I'm talking about choices like whether or not you are genuinely going to obey, trust, and listen to God instead of drowning Him out as you go about doing the same ol' things you *know* are getting you nowhere. We tend to go back to the things we know, just like Orpah did, and all that does is birth big giants in our life that are hard to take down. Choices matter. And they matter for eternity. It can mean the difference between living out God's purpose for your life and missing out on that purpose.

Always choose to follow God. *Always.* Because, yeah, it really does matter.

———————

Holy Father, guide me in all my
choices—especially the ones that can
pull me away from You. Amen.

94

So You Wanna Be a Hero

Faith is confidence in what we hope for and assurance about what we do not see.

HEBREWS 11:1

HEBREWS 11:1 IS A LIFE VERSE FOR ME. IT defines faith, and then the rest of Hebrews 11 goes through a long list of heroes of faith—Abraham, Sarah, Joseph, Moses, Rahab, Gideon, and others.

When we think about these heroes, it's easy to say, "I want that heroic kind of faith." Then we think we need to do heroic things. So we start asking God to give us something amazing to do. We think if He will just do that, we can be the kind of hero we read about in the Bible. But as I've studied the Bible, I've come to realize that the only thing separating us from the heroes of the Bible is faith. Being heroic is not about whether we do some amazing thing for Him. It's about having the faith and willingness to follow Him no matter what He asks of us.

Having faith and trusting God with all your heart are what make you a hero. If God gives you an assignment—whether it's speaking His Word to a stadium full of people, talking to a few people in a village in Africa, throwing a garage sale and giving the money to the church mission, paying for the coffee of the person behind you, showing up for a hurting friend, or simply texting encouragement to someone who needs it—and you obey it, that's what makes you a hero.

What I'm talking about here is kingdom-minded thinking and living. If you are a follower of God, then you are a part of His kingdom here on earth. You don't just have a purpose in heaven; you have a role to play right here and now. We need to surrender the idea of our own goal, our own dream, and our own heroic act and say, "God, I believe that whatever You say is not only good enough for me but is actually the perfect thing for my life. And it is going to bless more people than anything I could have thought of myself." That's kingdom-minded thinking, and that's truly heroic.

So . . . do you wanna be a hero?

Lord, I do believe in You, and I do want
to follow You in every part of my life.
Help me to be a hero of faith by obeying
You in every way, every day. Amen.

95

To Strive or Not to Strive?

My God will use his wonderful riches in Christ Jesus to give you everything you need.

PHILIPPIANS 4:19 NCV

IF YOU LISTEN TO MANY OF MY TALKS, YOU'LL probably notice that I say a lot about striving—and often in a negative way. So maybe you're wondering, *Does Sadie have something against working hard for what you want or for what God wants you to do?* Absolutely not! But I do believe there are two kinds of striving, and too often I find myself doing the wrong kind.

Here's how that can look in my life: When *I* have an opportunity to do something big, something that's going to require a lot of effort on my part, *I* can get pretty worked up about it. Especially if it's something *I* feel called by God to do. So *I* start thinking about all *I* need to do to make this opportunity work. *I* start making lists and planning and practicing. *I* start reading and researching. *I* end up thinking about it all the time and getting so anxious that *I* can't focus when I'm awake and *I* can't sleep. Because deep down *I* know *I* can't do it all on my own. That's the bad kind of striving. Why? Because *I* am depending on my own strength and ability instead of God's. (Notice all the *I*'s?) I need to remember that if God has called me to do something, He will give me everything I need to do it (2 Corinthians 9:8).

Does that mean I just sit back and do nothing? No, that's not how faith works. I still need to do my part, but I also need to trust God to do His part.

How can you know whether your "striving" for the Lord is the right kind? Ask yourself these questions: Are you stressed? Are your thoughts whirling around so much that you end up staring at the ceiling instead of sleeping? Are the *I*'s in your thoughts outnumbering your thoughts about God? If so, it's time for a heart-to-heart with God. Check in and make sure you're trusting in *His* strength and power, not your own. Because when we're in the middle of God's will for our lives and trusting in Him, He will give us everything we need to accomplish what He has called us to do.

Holy Father, when I'm relying on myself
instead of You, remind me to cease striving,
to be still, and to rest in You. Amen.

96

Totally Possible

[Abraham] was fully convinced that God is able to do whatever he promises.

ROMANS 4:21 NLT

IF YOU'RE ALIVE, THEN YOU'RE NOT DEAD. That's pretty obvious, right? But here's something a lot of us miss: if you're alive, then God's got plans and a purpose for you.

Now the thing is, God's plans might not always make sense to you. They might even seem downright impossible. But God is able to do the impossible.

Remember Abraham? You might know him from the Sunday-school song "Father Abraham." Well, he didn't start out that way. In fact, Abraham wasn't even his name at first. When God gave him the promise that He would make him into "a great nation" (Genesis 12:2), he was called Abram. The name *Abram* means "exalted father," but he was seventy-five years old and didn't have a single child, much less "a great nation" of descendants. Sometimes it feels like that with our calling, doesn't it? We feel like we've been called to *something*, but nothing around us looks any different.

Ten years later, God reminded Abram of His promise and said his heirs would be like the stars—too many to count (Genesis 15:4-6). Even more years passed, and God again promised Abram a son.[1] That's when He changed his name from *Abram* to *Abraham*, which means "father of many." By this point, Abraham was ninety-nine years old, and his wife, Sarah, was ninety (Genesis 17:1-5, 17)!

So let's sum this up: God promised to make a great nation out of a couple who not only had no children but were too old to even have children. Seems impossible, doesn't it? Not for God! Abraham and Sarah did have a son, and their descendants really are too many to count.

Abraham's age didn't matter. Sarah's age didn't matter. And even though they didn't follow God perfectly (Genesis 16, 20), God kept His promise. That's what we need to remember: no matter your age, no matter your past mistakes, no matter how impossible it might seem, God has a plan and a purpose for your life. Stick with Him, and He will keep His promises to you.

Holy Father, even though I don't always
see or understand Your plan for me, I
will trust You to lead me. Amen.

97

Dancing Past the Awkwardness

God has given each of you a gift from his great variety of spiritual gifts. Use them well to serve one another.

1 PETER 4:10 NLT

THE FIRST TIME I VISITED A JUVENILE DETENTION center, I was just there to watch from afar, not to teach or anything. Even so, when those girls walked in, I felt instantly intimidated! And the more intimidated I feel, the more awkward I get. So that day, I reverted to a lesson from the movie *Madagascar*: "Just smile and wave, boys. Smile and wave."[1]

No one smiled and waved back.

I remember feeling sorry for the teacher because no one was listening. Suddenly the group leader walked over to me and said, "Sadie, you have the anointing of a dance party! Get up there and start a dance party."

That's hilarious, I thought. *No way I'm about to do that. I hope she's kidding.*

Y'all, the woman was not kidding. She took the microphone and said, "Girls, this is Sadie, and she is going to start a dance party."

At first, I was shocked. Then I just went for it and tried to make a message for this moment. I said, "Here's the thing. We are all just daughters, which makes us sisters. And sisters are supposed to help each other feel like they belong. Now, I don't know what y'all like to do with your sisters, but I like to dance!"

Then I proceeded to do the weirdest dances I could think of. At first it was incredibly awkward, then one of the girls asked, "Sadie, do you know how to do the bunny hop?" I did not, which gave them the perfect opportunity to teach me. Soon, every single girl was doing the bunny hop, smiling and laughing. Sometimes you have to humble yourself and meet people where they are.

I still don't know if there's such a thing as a dance-party anointing, but let me say this: in life, to get to your anointing—to whatever purpose God has called, gifted, and empowered you to do—you have to get past the awkwardness you feel and the awkward looks people give you. And sometimes, you just have to dance.

_____

Lord, give me the courage to not let feeling awkward or foolish keep me from using the gifts You have given me. I humble myself to exalt Your name. Amen.

At Least You're Not Plankton

It is God who works in you to will and to act in order to fulfill his good purpose.

PHILIPPIANS 2:13

WE HAVE A SAYING IN MY FAMILY: "AT LEAST you're not plankton." Crazy, right? It's what we say when something bad happens or someone has a high-stress, "the world hates me" kind of day. It's our own unique take on the "at least you're not that guy" saying. Because plankton are pretty much the lowest of the low, right? Seriously. Just google it.

I had been saying this quote for a while when, one day, I felt the Spirit of God breathe a question in my spirit: *What if you were plankton? Could you still find purpose and passion? Are plankton really the lowest of the low?*

I sensed that God was trying to teach me something, so I set out to understand as much as I could about these microscopic organisms called plankton. First, I found that the word *plankton* comes from the Greek word *planktos*, which means "wanderer." So plankton are wanderers. Hmm . . . kind of like you and me.

I also learned that unlike other fish, some types of plankton swim vertically. This may not seem like a big deal until you understand that swimming vertically enables plankton to provide about 90 percent of the ocean's photosynthesis. Let me give you a little science refresher. PhotosynthesisEducation.com (yep, there's a whole website dedicated to it) says that photosynthesis is the process that plants use to make two important things: food and oxygen. I also learned that "photosynthesis is so essential to life on earth that most living organisms, including humans, cannot survive without it."[1] Not only that, these little plankton guys are also providing 50 percent of the oxygen you're breathing right now.[2]

What's my point? The world of the sea is so extraordinary and so complex, but God is so detailed and so amazing that even tiny, microscopic organisms have a purpose in His plan. It is easy for us to judge the significance—or insignificance—of someone else's purpose based on the world's standards of what looks impressive. But even though plankton are usually invisible to the human eye, their purpose is huge. If God can breathe purpose into the life of plankton, just imagine what He can do with your life.

———

Holy Father, You have told me that You have a purpose for my life. Guide me in that purpose, and help me to bring glory to Your name. Amen.

99

That's Not the Way
I Planned It

Many are the plans in a person's heart, but it is the Lord's purpose that prevails.

PROVERBS 19:21

DO YOU EVER FIND YOURSELF THINKING, *That's not the way I planned it*? It happens to me all the time. Seriously. *All. The. Time.* But I'm realizing it's often because God has something else in mind.

Like when I tried out for the cheerleading squad in high school. All of my friends were trying out, so I did too. I trained hard for the tryouts because that's what I do. I work for what I want, and I usually get what I'm going after. But not this time. I gave it all I had, but I still didn't make the squad. Yeah, it was sad, and I was embarrassed. I was the only one of my friends who didn't make the team.

Then my friends who did make the squad went to cheer camp. They were nervous because they knew the competition would be tough. Honestly, at first, I was a little jealous. Then it hit me: I had a choice to make. I could throw myself a pity party, or I could help my friends. I ended up making these crazy videos and texting them to my friends each day of their camp. I wanted to show them I was cheering for them back home. It actually made me feel like I was a part of their week. And ultimately that was the year our family's show took off, so being on the cheer team on top of that would not have been the best idea.

This is an example from when I was in high school, but this lesson—that things will not always go as planned—set me up for my future. There were jobs that did not pan out, experiences that weren't what I thought they would be, and moves to cities where things didn't always go how I wanted. What looks like a failure could actually be God's protection. Sometimes we can't control how life plays out, but our response is in our control.

Remember, your purpose isn't just about you. It's about building up His kingdom. When things don't go as planned, look for how God might be using you to do something for Him—like building up your friends. Because sometimes, living your best life is really about helping someone else live theirs.

Lord, when things don't go the way I planned, remind me to look for Your plans—and to trust that they are better than mine. Amen.

100

A Prayer for You

May you have the power to understand, as all God's people should, how wide, how long, how high, and how deep his love is.

EPHESIANS 3:18 NLT

HERE'S SOMETHING I HOPE FOR YOU: I WANT you to experience all that God wants to pour into your life—His presence, peace, love, joy, and purpose for your life. And you begin to experience God when you accept the call to follow Him and believe Jesus is His Son and that He came to save you from your sins. It continues when you step into the life God is calling you to live. That means praying the hard prayers and being ready to take a step when He sends you. Wherever you are on your journey with God, I want you to know that I am praying for you.

> Father God, thank You for loving us so much that You sent Your Son to save us. Thank You for coming to earth and dying on the cross to forgive our sins. Today, Lord, help us to lay down our lives, our wills, and our agendas and to

live for You and You alone. Send Your Spirit into our hearts and guide us every day. Show us the places in our lives where sin still lives and help us to deal with it quickly.

Open our eyes to see the call that You've placed on each of our lives. Help us to lay aside the fears, the shame, the doubts, and the mistakes of the past and to say to You, "Here I am, Lord, with no more limits on what You can do and no more distractions that take away my focus from You. Send me!"

Teach us and equip us to step into that call. Give us the faith to believe You really are going to do all that You've promised You will do. Open our hearts to the truth that we are loved, that we are cherished, and that we are never alone because You are always right beside us.

I know You have a plan for our lives, Lord, and that You are walking with us toward the realization of that plan and purpose. Let our lives bring glory to You and more people to Your kingdom.

Amen.

Notes

Devotion 11: The Overwhelmed

1. Craig Groeschel, "God with Us in the Wilderness," Sermons.love, accessed February 9, 2021, https://sermons.love/craig-groeschel/4339-craig-groeschel -god-with-us-in-the-wilderness.html.

Devotion 19: Not a Copy

1. Lexico.com, s.v. "original," accessed October 18, 2019, https://www.lexico.com /en/definition/original.

Devotion 20: As Real as It Gets

1. Amanda MacMillan, "Why Instagram Is the Worst Social Media for Mental Health," *Time*, May 25, 2017, https://time.com/4793331/instagram-social -media-mental-health/.

Devotion 26: Born to Be Royal

1. *The Princess Diaries*, directed by Garry Marshall, featuring Anne Hathaway (Mia Thermopolis) and Heather Matarazzo (Lilly Moscovitz), released July 29, 2001, Walt Disney Pictures.

Devotion 47: Keep Moving Forward

1. Christine Caine (@ChristineCaine), Twitter, November 20, 2019, 4:00 p.m., https://twitter.com/ChristineCaine/status/1197273481970253825.

Devotion 48: Slap Fear in the Face

1. Will Smith, "What Skydiving Taught Me About Fear," YouTube, April 26, 2018, https://www.youtube.com/watch?v=bFIB05LGtMs.

Devotion 54: If You're Carrying the Football . . .

1. "Rick Warren: Hardest Criticism to Swallow Is Claim That All Megachurches Are the Same," *Christian Today*, accessed February 10, 2021, https:// christiantoday.com.au/news/rick-warren-criticism-hardest-to-swallow-is -claim-that-all-megachurches-are-the-same.html.

Devotion 57: It's Just Being Happy

1. *Collins Dictionary*, s.v. "celebrate," accessed October 17, 2019, https://www .collinsdictionary.com/dictionary/english/celebrate.

Devotion 60: Just Four Words

1. *Merriam-Webster*, s.v. "fill the gaps," accessed October 17, 2019, https://www.merriam-webster.com/dictionary/fill%20the%20gaps.
2. TheFreeDictionary.com, s.v. "fill the gap," accessed October 17, 2019, https://idioms.thefreedictionary.com/fill+the+gaps.

Devotion 69: What It Means to Truly Live

1. Lexico.com, s.v. "live," accessed May 4, 2020, https://www.lexico.com/definition/live.
2. Lexico.com, s.v. "remain," accessed May 4, 2020, https://www.lexico.com/definition/remain.

Devotion 88: One Really Big Fear

1. Tim Elmore, "6 Fears and Concerns of College Students Today," Growing Leaders, May 31, 2012, http://growingleaders.com/blog/6-fears-and-concerns-of-college-students-today.

Devotion 93: Yeah, It Really Does Matter

1. Tamar Meir, "Orpah: Midrash and Aggadah," The Encyclopedia of Jewish Women, Jewish Women's Archive, February 27, 2009, https://jwa.org/encyclopedia/article/orpah-midrash-and-aggadah.

Devotion 96: Totally Possible

1. Bruce N. Cameron, "Abram and Sarah: Faith Tested and Tried," GoBible.org, accessed November 2, 2020, http://www.gobible.org/study/459.php.

Devotion 97: Dancing Past the Awkwardness

1. *Madagascar*, directed by Eric Darnell and Tom McGrath, released May 27, 2005, DreamWorks Animation.

Devotion 98: At Least You're Not Plankton

1. "Photosynthesis for Kids," Photosynthesis Education, accessed November 2, 2020, https://photosynthesiseducation.com/photosynthesis-for-kids/.
2. Amy Hansen, "Invisible Watery World," Ask a Biologist, Arizona State University School of Life Sciences, accessed November 2, 2020, https://askabiologist.asu.edu/explore/plankton.

About the Author

SADIE ROBERTSON HUFF, FIRST INTRODUCED
to the world as a star of A&E's *Duck Dynasty* and ABC's *Dancing with the Stars*, recognized she could be a positive voice to those in need of an inspiring presence in their lives, and she's become one of the most prominent voices of her generation. Sadie's passion is to speak, to write, and to encourage. She is a sister and friend to more than five million followers on her various social platforms, which she sees as a direct line of communication to her peers.

Sadie's creative and entrepreneurial spirit has helped her launch her Live Original brand, which speaks to millions across her various platforms, including YouTube, social media, the *Live Original* blog, the LO Fam Community, the Live Original tour, and her *Whoa That's Good* podcast.

Additionally, Sadie has long poured her heart into philanthropic efforts. She has loved partnering with Roma Boots, Help One Now, World Vision, and the World Food Program over the last few years. To date, Sadie has been able to be a voice and agent of change in many countries, including Peru, Somalia, Moldova, and the Dominican Republic.

Sadie is married to the man of her dreams, Christian, and continues to learn what it means to truly live and celebrate in every moment of life.